Francis Carolus Eeles

The Church and other Bells of Kincardineshire

being a complete account of all the bells in the county, their history, uses,

and ornaments - with notices of their founders, and an article on the more

interesting belfries

Francis Carolus Eeles

The Church and other Bells of Kincardineshire

being a complete account of all the bells in the county, their history, uses, and ornaments - with notices of their founders, and an article on the more interesting belfries

ISBN/EAN: 9783337272906

Printed in Europe, USA, Canada, Australia, Japan

Cover: Foto ©Lupo / pixelio.de

More available books at **www.hansebooks.com**

THE

CHURCH AND OTHER BELLS

OF

KINCARDINESHIRE

BEING A COMPLETE ACCOUNT OF ALL THE BELLS IN THE COUNTY,
THEIR HISTORY, USES, AND ORNAMENTS; WITH NOTICES OF
THEIR FOUNDERS, AND AN ARTICLE ON THE MORE
INTERESTING BELFRIES.

TO WHICH IS PREFIXED

A SHORT GENERAL SURVEY

OF

BELLS IN SCOTLAND,

BY
F. C. EELES.

WITH ILLUSTRATIONS.

REPRINTED, WITH ADDITIONS, FROM THE "ABERDEEN ECCLESIOLOGICAL SOCIETY'S TRANSACTIONS."

ABERDEEN: W. JOLLY & SONS.
LONDON: ELLIOT STOCK, 62 PATERNOSTER ROW, E.C.

CONTENTS.

	PAGE
PREFACE.	
ADDITIONS AND CORRECTIONS.	
INTRODUCTION.	
1. ON SCOTCH BELLS GENERALLY,	1
2. ON KINCARDINESHIRE BELLS,	13
FULL DESCRIPTION OF EVERY BELL IN KINCARDINESHIRE,	22
(In alphabetical order of Parishes).	
BELFRIES.	
1. GENERAL,	40
2. KINCARDINESHIRE,	41
APPENDIX.	
1. MEDIAEVALS OF DOUBTFUL ORIGIN,	44
2. LIST OF BOOKS ON THE BELLS OF VARIOUS ENGLISH COUNTIES,	44
3. EXPLANATION OF TECHNICAL TERMS,	45
4. LETTERS, &C., RELATING TO THE ST. CYRUS BELLS,	45
5. IRISH AND ENGLISH FOUNDRIES,	48

PLATES.

1. ORNAMENTS AND LETTERING USED BY OSTENS OF ROTTERDAM; FROM BANCHORY TERNAN AND KINNEFF.
   LOW COUNTRY ORNAMENT FROM 1ST OF ST. JAMES'S, STONE-
   HAVEN, ... Frontispiece.
2. BELFRIES AT FETTERESSO AND NIGG.
   MEDIAEVAL BELL AT STRACHAN.
   ORNAMENTS, FOUNDRY MARK, &C., USED BY GELY OF OLD ABER-
   DEEN, ... facing p. 14.
3. ORNAMENTS AND LETTERING USED BY THE LATER OLD ABERDEEN
   FOUNDERS; FROM SKENE, NIGG, AND DUNNOTTAR, facing p. 16
4. BELL TURRETS AT ARBUTHNOTT, ... facing p. 22
5. BELFRIES AT KINNEFF, GARVOC, AND INVERBERVIE (OLD CH.), facing p. 40
6. TYPICAL ENGLISH BELL AND HANGINGS, . . . facing p. 45
7. MODERN ENGLISH PEAL HUNG FOR CHANGE-RINGING, facing p. 48

PREFACE.

In the following pages an attempt has been made to do for a county in Scotland what has been done for several in England with such successful results. The work has been carried out on the lines favoured by English Ecclesiologists, only such modifications being introduced as experience suggested or as the altered circumstances of the case appeared to render necessary. For example, while English books on bells are usually restricted to a consideration of those of the Parish Churches, it has in the present instance been deemed advisable to notice not only the bells of other places of worship, but also such as occur in municipal and private possession. Cases like Dundee and Crail showed from the first that in Scotland town bells would always have to receive notice. But the work of investigation had not gone far before the writer found that the circumstances of the country made it very hard to know where to draw the line in matters ecclesiastical, with the result that he thought it better to include all bells rather than run the risk of excluding any that were of value.

As so little is known about Scotch bells, an introduction has been prefixed which treats of the matter at some length, the object being to bring into a readily accessible form all the information at present obtainable on the subject, besides the results of the author's own observations. It is hoped by this means to furnish a foundation for future work, and also to stimulate interest in an at present obscure subject by showing from examples how many attractions it possesses.

The parish boundaries as they existed at the Revolution have as far as possible been followed, and the parishes have been arranged in alphabetical order. In cases where they are not coterminous with the counties, the rule is followed that overlapping portions be included in the county in which the Parish Church is situated.

All ancient sites are specified whether they have bells or not; so are all Episcopal and Roman Catholic Churches; other places of worship are only mentioned when they have bells.

In the description of each bell, unless otherwise stated, the bell has canons, and the inscription is round the shoulder. The single letter refers to the approximate place of the note in the musical scale (Soc. of Arts Pitch), the size is the diameter at the mouth, and the times given are the times of ringing; "s" prefixed denoting a service to follow. Inscriptions have been rendered as nearly as possible in facsimile; consequently any irregularities that may appear are not printers' errors as might at first be supposed, but have been advisedly reproduced from the bells themselves.

The appendix contains an article on the more interesting belfries in the county; also a series of brief historical notes on the English founders whose work is to be met with in Scotland. One firm of founders has been kind enough to lend two blocks showing a typical English bell as hung for change ringing and a third showing a peal of eight with several of the bells "up." These, together with a few explanatory remarks also find a place in the appendix.

It only remains to express thanks to all who have in any way assisted the author in his work. These are far too numerous to mention individually, and he is reluctantly compelled to deny himself this satisfaction. He can simply express his warm appreciation of the kindness and consideration he has received.

This cannot, however, free him from the obligation of acknowledging his special indebtedness to the President and other members of the Aberdeen Ecclesiological Society, who have interested themselves so much in his behalf. The Rev. D. G. Barron, Minister of Dunnottar, and Mr. J. A. Henderson, Cults, have rendered valuable assistance. To the Very Rev. The Dean of Brechin, and to Mr. De Lessert, Aberdeen, he is likewise much indebted. Nor ought he to omit the names of Mr. A. H. Cocks, of Gt. Marlow, Bucks., and Mr. W. H. J. Weale, Librarian at South Kensington.

Messrs. Gillet & Johnston of Croydon, Mears & Stainbank of London, J. Murphy of Dublin, J. Taylor & Co. of Loughborough, J. Warner & Sons of Spitalfields, J. C. Wilson & Co. of Glasgow, Vickers Sons & Co. of Sheffield, besides other founders, have all been most obliging in affording every information in their power.

F. C. E.

STONEHAVEN,
January, 1897.

ADDITIONS AND CORRECTIONS.

Page 3, line 25. The Strachan bell should be included among the *Later* Mediaevals.
- „ 5, note 2, line 7. For "Suffolk" read "Cambridgeshire."
- „ 5, note 3, line 2. For "1837" read "1873."
- „ 6, line 19. For "Burgherhuys" read "Burgerhuys."
- „ 7, line 24. For "prove" read "proves."
- „ 8, line 10. For "evidently............was........." read "in a few cases possibly a Low Mass, there being.........."
- „ 8, line 15. Delete "Here......being" and read "we find the bell rung at 9 for Matins."
- „ 8, line 23. For "theirsel" read "theirsels."
- „ 16, line 43. For "had" read "have."
- „ 19, note 2. For "inscripion" read "inscription."
- „ 20. Table of Times of Ringing, under "Banchory Devenic," add "8 a.m. (discontinued)."
- „ 21. Table of Times of Ringing of Town Bells, add "Bervie (discontiued), 6 a.m., 9 a.m., 2 p.m., 9 p.m. exc. Suns."
- „ 22. Arbuthnott, S. Mary's Chapel. Peattie; add "Site doubtful."
- „ 26, line 4. Delete "6 p.m."
- „ 29. Inscription on Cowie Sanctus Bell should be in letters like that of Banchory Devenic Free Church, p. 24.
- „ 32. S. John the Baptist, Drumlithie; since inscription was printed, the bell has been recast with the following inscription:—

    1834

on waist   RECAST BY MEARS & STAINBANK, LONDON 1897.

INTRODUCTION.

I. ON SCOTCH BELLS GENERALLY AS FAR AS HITHERTO INVESTIGATED.

ONE of the lesser results of the Catholic revival in England has been the increasing recognition of the importance of Church History, Antiquities, and Architecture—in a word—of Ecclesiology. And one branch of Ecclesiology which has received special attention is the study of Church Bells, their history, uses, and artistic merits.[1]

The origin of bells is involved in obscurity, and as much has been written on the subject, there is no necessity to enlarge upon it here.

The introduction of Christianity into these islands almost certainly took place at the beginning of the Christian era, and, coming directly from the East, probably brought bells with it. Thus no musical instrument can be said to have been so long or so closely identified with the service of the Church as the bell.

The Celtic and other early bells have been dealt with elsewhere; so has the development of the present form of bell. We may therefore turn at once to the part of the subject that concerns us, namely, bells since the early middle ages. Much thought and care have at various times been given to the casting, tuning, and ornamentation of bells. Bell-founding is an art in the truest sense of the term, and has been recognised as such, at least in England, where the antiquarian and artistic value of bells has met with due appreciation. Many Ecclesiologists have made them a special study, and have given us exhaustive accounts of those in several of the English counties. Besides its historical and educational use, such work has often been the means of averting the destruction of valuable property, and of perpetuating the memory of many specimens of bell-founding, which for one reason or another have been destroyed.[2]

Surely it is time that something of the kind were done in Scotland, which, despite all adverse influences, still contains many bells of surpassing interest.

Before proceeding to speak more particularly of the Kincardineshire bells, it will be well to give a brief account of what little is known of bells in Scotland generally. And first it will be necessary to consider the position of Scotland in regard to methods of ringing, as this will often give a reason for the kind of work we meet with.

In the early Middle ages—not only in Scotland but also in England and on the Continent—the richer churches each possessed several bells, obtained usually at various times, and often without regard to their respective sizes or to the relations

---

[1] No especial name has as yet been given to this study. *Campanology* denotes exclusively the science of change-ringing, while what is discussed here is the comparative study of bells.

[2] For a list of works on the bells of the various English counties, see Appendix.

between their notes. The great bell was often dedicated to the patron saint of the church, and the smaller bells to the other saints who were commemorated in the church below; each was used separately for the services at the corresponding altar, while all were used for High Mass and on great occasions. A desire to ring the bells in a musical way made itself felt very early. On the Continent this took the form of adding a carillon to the already existing collection of heavy bells, while in England it showed itself in a tendency to make the heavy bells themselves form a part of the diatonic scale, and therefore suitable for ringing in succession. Shortly before the Reformation the carillon developed very rapidly on the Continent, and it reached its perfection in the Seventeenth century. It consisted of a large number of small light bells, fixed "dead," and sounded by hammers worked by wires from an arrangement of levers, something like the keys of an organ.[1]

In England the carillon was unknown, and each bell there was rung by a rope attached either to a lever at right angles to the stock, or to a quarter or half wheel. This means that they were not "rung" at all, in the strictest sense, but were only chimed. There seem grounds for supposing that this was done in changing rotation, though only at the caprice of the ringers. In the Seventeenth century real change ringing came into vogue, and took the ringing world by storm; after the Restoration, indeed, it soon became a popular amusement. Bells were increased in size and weight, every church aiming at the possession of at least five or six, though we find that for this purpose the number never exceeded twelve. Whole wheels, heavier cages, and the necessary appliances for setting[2] the bells followed as a matter of course, and the English ring soon took the form in which we know it now. This change ringing, with its elaborate hangings and thick bells, was as unknown out of England as the carillon was in England, although at a later period it was to some extent introduced into Ireland.

It was, perhaps, due to the close political relations which existed between France and Scotland, that the latter has chiefly followed the Continental usage in preference to the English. That this was the case admits of no question, as the following considerations will show. We have part of a carillon left at Perth, and one cast at Edinburgh at the end of the Seventeenth century. Wherever there are more bells than one, except in absolutely modern rings from England, they are merely heterogeneous collections of the Continental type. Such are those at Perth, Forfar, and Montrose; at the last-mentioned place, indeed, and also at S. Andrews, Stirling and Arbroath, they still chime the bells with a simultaneous jangle after the true Continental fashion. In some cases, however, the bells form part of the diatonic scale, and are chimed in succession, as English bells were before the introduction of change-ringing. It may be noted that the latter system has been recently introduced in several places—as at S. Paul's (Ep. Ch.), Dundee, in 1872, and S. Mary's Cathedral (Ep.), Edinburgh, in 1879.

Such being the case, it is not surprising, when we turn to the bells themselves,

[1] The collection of heavy bells remained in addition to the carillon, and has never been superseded on the Continent.

[2] To set a bell is to turn it mouth upwards and allow it to rest in that position by the stay coming in contact with the slider and preventing its falling right over.

to find that the majority of the old ones were imported from the Low Countries, and that all those of native casting were mere copies of Low Country models: in fact, it is towards the end of the last century before we find the English model of bell in use at all.

In England, most of the really ancient rings have been recast during the last two hundred years, so as to fit them for change ringing. These heavy rings are of great interest, and for loudness and brilliancy of tone, as well as for accuracy of tune, are absolutely unsurpassed. For external artistic merit they cannot be compared to the mediaeval bells, and certainly not to the Continental. On their part, these Low Country bells, being only used for chiming, never reached the great strength of the English, but they are nearly always ornamented with a wonderful profusion of delicate borders and friezes, and in many cases with excellently modelled medallions and groups of figures, flowers, and fruit.

Low Country bells are almost entirely absent from England. Dr. Raven, mentioning a stray Flemish bell in Suffolk,[1] says "Flemish bells are so rare," and devotes two plates and several pages to matters connected with it, and the late Mr. J. C. L. Stahlschmidt, one of the greatest authorities on the subject who has ever lived, gives more space to a diminutive Dutch bell at Frindsbury[2] than to many a large peal. On the other hand, such bells are fairly common in this country, and herein, to a great extent, lies the peculiar interest of investigating Scotch bells.

Bells in Scotland may be divided into three distinct classes—Scotch, Low Country, and English, according to their origin. The first of these may, for convenience, be further sub-divided into the three following groups—Mediaeval, Renaissance, and Modern.

The Mediaeval probably includes, among the earlier work, the bell at Strachan and the 1st at Kirkwall Cathedral; and certainly the "minister's bell" of S. Giles', Elgin, by Thomas de Dunbar, 1402.[3]

Among later Mediaeval work, the 2nd, 3rd, and 4th (before recasting) of Kirkwall Cathedral were given by Bp. Maxwell, and cast by Robert Borthwyk in Edinburgh Castle, 1528. These have black letter inscriptions, capital and small, with the arms of Maxwell and a figure of S. Magnus; they are 33 and 37 in. in diameter.[4] A bell mentioned by Lukis[4] as the 1st of Lochmaben; the bell of Fowlis Easter, 1508; and that of Kirkmaiden, 1533, by one John Morison, are also later Mediaevals.

After the Mediaeval period, bell-founding everywhere entered upon a new era. In England, stimulated by the introduction of change-ringing, it was soon to blaze forth afresh, after having been damped down by the Reformation. On the Continent, the growth of the carillon and the fresh art of the Renaissance afforded opportunities of a new and varied character. It was only in Scotland that nothing was done, for here the Reformation put a complete stop to all kinds of work connected with ecclesiastical art, and in the subsequent wanton destruction and gross neglect, bells naturally suffered greatly.

[1] *Church Bells of Suffolk*, pp. 74-75.
[2] *Church Bells of Kent*, p. 88, &c.
[3] Young's *History of Elgin*.
[4] Lukis' *Account of Church Bells*, p. 134.

As an instance of the results of this we see, according to Dr. J. Robertson, *Scottish Abbeys and Cathedrals*, p. 101, that "Archbishop Abbot, whose Puritanism made him regard things in Scotland with no unfriendly eye, related to Sir Henry Spelman that, in 1605, he found only one bell[1] in Edinburgh, and that not only had the country churches no bells, but when, at Dunbar, he asked how they chanced to be without such a commodity, 'the minister, a crumpt unseemly person, thinking the question as strange, replied " It was one of the Reformed[2] Churches!"'"

We have an instance of wanton spoliation of Church property at the time of the reformation, apart from religious motives, in the Burgh Archives of Dundee, whence we learn that in 1560 the Baillies ordained "James Young to exhibit and produce before them the bell of Kynspindie, whilk was arrestit in his house to the effect they may do justice thereanent."

He failed in this and was required "to deliver to Archibald Dowglass of Kynspindie his bell or pay him the sum of twenty pounds."

Some months later they ordained "William Carmichell to deliver to the parochiners of Lyff their bell, taken by him frae certain persons wha wrangously intromittit therewith.[3]"

But towards the end of the Sixteenth century we find a very great improvement in such matters, and bells began to be obtained in large numbers from the Low Countries. These bells will be dealt with later on, as we must first glance at the native work. A few bells of the early part of the 17th century are to be met with; such are Glencairn, 1611, and also the works of Robert Hog, who had a foundry at Stirling, c. 1632-1639, and cast among others the bell of Killin. In the latter part of the century Scotch bells became more common, and we have foundries in working at Edinburgh and Aberdeen. The first named was carried on by John Meikle, who in 1698-9 was ordered by the Town Council's Committee to cast a carillon of 23 for S. Giles' Cathedral, Edinburgh. The famous "Kate Kennedy[4]" at the College Church, S. Andrews, was recast by him in 1686, and has ornaments and foundry marks copied from those of various Dutch founders. He seems to have been succeeded by Robert Maxwell, who cast one of the Peebles bells in 1714, the 2nd and 3rd of the old ring at S. Giles' Edinburgh, in 1728, and many others, among them a small bell at the College Church, St. Andrews, with rough irregular lettering, and one of the same Dutch borders that Meikle used. A William Ormiston of Edinburgh, who cast a bell for Carmyllie in 1748, was probably his successor, and seems to have been followed by John Milne, who cast the bell of Kilbirnie in 1753.[5]

---

[1] There were at least two.

[2] We may perhaps be excused for quoting the following passage from an old sermon of the period, which certainly is not wanting in force :—"The pretended Reformation of the Christian religion, which has lately come up from Hell, has not felt satisfied with its mad rage against the rites of the Catholic Church, unless it could also fasten its cursed hand and tooth upon the instruments (Bells), by which she is roused and called forth to piety and Divine worship, and could cast forth the venom of its cursing upon inanimate implements."

[3] *Old Dundee*, Alex. Maxwell, 1891, p. 164.

[4] So called because dedicated to S. Catharine, and given by Bishop Kennedy in 1460. It is a tub-shaped (31⅞ in.) bell with a short waist and flat crown and is now cracked and disused.

[5] *Parish Church of Kilbirnie*, J. S. Dobie, p. 25.

BELLS OF KINCARDINESHIRE.   5

The Aberdeen foundry was carried on by Patrick Kilgour in the Seventeenth century, and by Albert Gely, John Mowat, and Andrew Lawson in the Eighteenth. It will be mentioned at greater length later on.

This brings us to the modern period, when we begin to find bad imitations of Eighteenth century English work. Hitherto all the bells we have considered have been on the Low Country model, and have possessed at least some attempts at artistic ornamentation. But now we find all pretentions to artistic merit gone, and neither interest nor redeeming feature. Such bells only demand notice because an account of the bells of any county would otherwise be incomplete. The founders now become too numerous and insignificant to mention, as almost any brassfounder undertook work of the kind.[1]

Quite recently a number of bells have been cast by John C. Wilson & Co. of Gorbals Brass foundry, Glasgow, who first began to cast bells in 1838, when the foundry belonged to David Burges, who originated it. Among their more important bells are Townhead (54½ in., 33 cwt., 1866), Dunfermline Corporation Buildings (55 in., 33 cwt., 1879, E♭), Pollockshields (48 in., 25 cwt., 1884, F.), and the great bell of Glasgow Cathedral (48 in. 1896). This firm have also cast several sets of clock bells and a few peals, among them Lamlash 8, Wemyss Bay 8, Coatbridge Wesleyan Chapel 6.

The Low Country bells now claim our attention : they are the most important we have to do with, and, as already indicated, are almost unknown in England.[2]

Among Mediaevals, we have the 17th at Perth, a fine (33½ in.) Fourteenth century bell, with a very long waist and most delicate Lombardic lettering :[3] the 15th at Perth, a small (21½ in.) Fifteenth century bell with black letter inscription, and, until recast by Mears in 1836, the great bell of S. Giles' Cathedral, Edinburgh, by John and William Hoerken, 1460.

In the Sixteenth and Seventeenth centuries we find Low Country Bells becoming more numerous. Most of those of the Sixteenth century are by one or other of the Waghevens family. Henri Waghevens, who died in 1483, came of a very famous race of Mechlin founders, who did a great amount of work. There were several of this name ; Peter and George, sons of Henry, 1483-1520 ; Simon, who seems to have been

---

[1] Several of these will, however, be noticed in connection with Kincardineshire.
[2] The following seem to be all the foreign bells as yet found in England :—
Baschurch, Salop., 1447, by Jan Van Venloe (? from Valle Crucis). *Church Bells of Suffolk*, p. 74. Bitterly, Salop., the 3rd, with inscription in old French. *English Bells and Bell Lore*, T. North, p. 40. Bromeswell, Suff., the 1st, 1530, by Cornelis Waghevens. *Church Bells of Suffolk*, p. 74. Eglingham, Northumberland, 1489 (by a Waghevens ?) said to be from Berwick. *Bells of the Church*, Ellacombe. Frindsbury, Kent, the Sanctus bell, 1670, by Gerrit Schimmel of Deventer. *Church Bells of Kent*. Lavenheath, Suff., by Gerhard Horner of Stockholm. *Church Bells of Suffolk*. Norwich, S. Giles' Hospital, by Peter Van den Gheyn (?) *Church Bells of Norfolk*, p. 85. Tottenham, Middlesex, 1663, by "L.H." *History of Church of Allhallows, Tottenham*, Geo. Waight, 1876. Vowchurch, Herts. (till recently) by J. Van Venloe. *Church Bells of Suffolk*, p. 74, etc. Whitton, Suff., 1441, by Jan Van Venloe (?) *Church Bells of Suffolk*, p. 74, etc. Nicolaston, Glamorgan, 1518 (by G. Waghevens?) *Church Bells of Suffolk*, p. 74.
[3] Other Fourteenth century bells were one formerly at Dunning by John of Rotterdam, 1320 (*Dunning*; J. Wilson, 1837, pp. 12, 13), and the three given by Provost Leith to S. Nicholas, Aberdeen, 1351.

a younger brother, 1491-1516[1]; Medard, 1524-1557; Cornelis, whose earliest date is 1530; Jacop, whose earliest date is 1542 and latest 1554,[2] in addition to a later Jacop, c. 1590.

There were also a Giles Waghevens, c. 1514-1515, and a Jacques Waghevens, c. 1542-1547.

The great (53 in.) bell of Perth, highly ornamented, with an elaborate founder's mark and a projecting statue, is a fine example of the work of Peter Waghevens, 1506. The old bell at Kettins, 1519, the 1st at Dunning, 1526, which has two good medallions, and part of a carillon at Perth, 1526, are the work of George (Jooris) Waghevens, who also cast the 3rd, 4th and 5th of the vast peal formerly at King's College, Aberdeen, and also a 57 in. bell formerly at Perth. Jacop Waghevens cast the clock bell formerly at Glasgow Cathedral in 1554.

The Van den Gheyns were a long line of Louvain and Mechlin founders, and cast many famous bells for the Low Country churches. Their successors are said to be Andre Louis J. Van Aerschodt and Severin Van Aerschodt, sons of a daughter of Matthias Van den Gheyn (1721-1785), the famous organist and carillioneur. An early 16th century bell at Culsalmond, is by Peter Van den Gheyn. Those of Inverarity and Crail, both 1614, are by a later Peter Van den Gheyn.

We find the work of Jan Burgherhuys at Melrose, 1608, Fyvie, 1609, and elsewhere. That of Michael Burgerhuys his successor ranges from 1617 at Lundie to 1647 at Smailholm. It includes the bell of Rutherglen, 1635, with many others, not least of which was the old "S. Lawrence" of S. Nicholas, Aberdeen, recast by him in 1634. This splendid bell was unfortunately broken in pieces on the occasion of the destruction of the spire by fire in 1874, and its fragments were sold as old metal and now lie in a cellar. Michael's successor, a younger Jan Burgerhuys, cast the bells of Farnell in 1662, Panbride in 1664, and Liff in 1696. These were Middelburg founders, and they used a Phoenix for their foundry mark.

Turning to the Rotterdam founders we have Cornelis Ouderogge[3] and Peter Ostens in the Seventeenth century, and John Spicht in the Eighteenth, with perhaps others. The 4th at Kirkwall Cathedral was recast in 1682 by an Amsterdam founder, Cladius Fremy.[4] Another Amsterdam bell, by Gerhard Koster, 1663, was formerly at Calton Church, Glasgow. Peter Jansen cast the bells of Midmar, 1642, Rathen, 1643, and Auchterless, 1644; Andreas Ehem cast that of Rescobie, 1620, and one " I. M." that of Oathlaw in 1618; the Strichen bell 1633, and one formerly at Dunfermline Tolbooth, 1654[5] are by Henrick Ter Horst of Deventer, and are of importance be-

---

[1] According to Dr. Raven, *Church Bells of Suffolk*, but there is a bell at S. Jacques, Bruges, by a Simon Waghevens, 1525 (W. H. J. Weale; *Bruges et ses Environs*, 1864).

[2] According to Dr. Raven, but we find bells by a Jacop Waghevens in 1560 and 1561.

[3] Cast 2nd at Forfar, 1637; Navar, 1655 (now in Arbroath Museum); 3rd at Stirling, 1657. His foundry mark seems to have been a sort of star, and he used very thick letters in high relief. Ostens was probably his successor.

[4] Lukis' *Account of Church Bells*, p. 134.

[5] *Annals of Dunfermline*; Ebenezer Henderson, p. 328.

cause Stahlschmidt,[1] speaking of a small bell by Gerrit Schimmel of Deventer, 1670, says, "I do not think a specimen from a Deventer foundry has been found before."

At Cowan's Hospital, Stirling, there is a bell by Adam Danckwart, 1665, showing part of the same frieze that Dr. Raven found on the Bromeswell bell.

There is a bell at Monifieth by Jacop Ser, 1554, inscribed in French, and one at Comrie, 1583, inscribed in German.

Although not from the Low Countries the great bell of Forfar must be noticed here. This very remarkable bell is one mass of inscription and ornament, and was cast in 1656 by Gert Meyer of Stockholm. It is 45 in. in diameter, and has large ornamental borders round both soundbow and shoulder, and a beautiful figure of S. Michael and the Dragon, besides other decorations.

In recent times we have a carillon of 43 cast in 1886 for S. Nicholas, Aberdeen, by Severin Van Aerschodt of Louvaine, who also cast a peal of 9 for Lower Beeding, Sussex, in 1887.

Before turning to the English bells we must notice a bell at Blairs College by J. Murphy of Dublin, 1859, who in the same year recast the 3rd of the famous peal of Limerick Cathedral.

English bells form a very large subject, as there is a considerable amount of information on which to draw. We will of course confine ourselves merely to such as are found in Scotland.

We are doubtful if among them there are any Mediaevals, though specimens of this class may yet be forthcoming in the Southern counties. The character of the inscriptions[2] on the 1st and 2nd of the ring formerly at King's College, Aberdeen, almost prove them to have been English, but they are now destroyed. The bell at the West Church, Greenock, 1677, seems to be English, and so does that at Fetteresso, 1736, but English bells of any kind are not common until quite the end of the 18th century, when the old Scotch founders had all died out. Thenceforward they become more numerous, and since the beginning of the present century, with the exception of those by Wilson of Glasgow, almost every bell of any size has been brought from England.

Most of these have come from the Whitechapel Foundry, which had almost a monopoly until the middle of the present century, when other foundries came into prominence. Of these last, that of J. Taylor & Co. of Loughborough seems to have done most work for Scotland.

Some of these English Foundries—notably that at Whitechapel—have long and interesting histories, and much might be said of the bells they have cast. But as the foundries whose work we are concerned with in Scotland have been well and carefully dealt with by English writers, it is unnecessary to do more than mention them here.

Methods of ringing have been dealt with above, but something must be said here about customs—that is, about ringing at peculiar times and on special occasions. Many of the ancient customs such as yet remain in England have in

---

[1] *Church Bells of Kent*, p. 88.
[2] 1st—Trinitate sacra fiat haec campana beata. 2nd—Protege precor pia quos convoco Sancta Maria.

Scotland either died out or else been prohibited, but still there are several peculiar uses which are undoubted survivals, and demand special attention.

These are the times of the ringing of church bells (apart from immediately before services), and to a less extent, the times of ringing of town bells.

In many parishes the practice still remains of ringing the bell at 8 A.M. or some other early hour, long before the time of the present service, and the hours at which this is done often give a clue to the times of the Mediaeval services, being in point of fact the ringing for them.

In some churches the bell is rung at 8 and 10, the service being later. Here the first is probably the Matins bell, and the second the Mass bell—evidently a Low Mass, it being perhaps probable that there was also a High Mass later. Those places where the bell is rung at 10 only are usually of this class, the 8 o'clock ringing having been discontinued.

In other churches, apparently those which are more out of the way, or of less importance, we find the bell rung at 9. Here there was probably only one Mass, the 9 o'clock bell being for Matins. In these cases the Mass would have been about 11, hence there is no 10 o'clock bell, and the Mass bell does not remain separate from the modern service bell, where that service is not very late; where, however, it is late, the Mass bell does remain, being usually rung at 11, and occasionally at 10.30.

At the present day, various reasons, more or less utilitarian, have been given for these old service bells. The country people say that the 8 o'clock bell is to "let ye ken it's the Sabbath," or to "gar the hill-folk mak' theirsel ready or the Kirk win in."

This is very often called the "rousing bell," and the later bell the "dressing bell," or the "get ready." A more important reason sometimes given for these later ringings is that they are the survival of the ringing-in to a Scripture reading, which in Presbyterian times was introduced before the regular service to prevent the "profanation of the Sabbath" by any chance conversation that might take place between those who had arrived at the Kirk too early. This was extremely common, but it seems more likely that it helped to perpetuate the older custom than that it was the cause of the introduction of a new one. We must also remember that there was no Scripture reading to urge as the reason for the 8 o'clock bell.

That these early ringings then, are the survivals of the ancient services seems to admit of no question, but it is uncertain which services belonged to each, and the suggestions put forth above can be but tentative, seeing the extremely limited amount of information there is on the subject. A great difficulty is caused by the various modifications that have been made in recent times for the sake of convenience, and to suit the late risers of more modern days.[1] It is highly probable,

---

[1] Perth Session Records, July 10, 1560. "The session, after the appointment of the order of communication ordains that the first bell should be rung at four in the morning; the second at half five o'clock; the third at five. The second ministration, the first bell to be rung at half nine o'clock; the second at nine; the third at half ten." July 6, 1703. "The session appoints that the church doors be opened at seven of the clock in the morning and *not* till then; as also that the first bell be rung at eight of the clock the second at half nine and the third at nine." At Elgin in the early part of the Seventeenth century the bell was rung at 3.30 a.m. on Communion Sundays, the service being at 5 or 6.

however, that were the times of ringing throughout the country carefully collected and arranged, it would be quite possible to reconstruct a fairly correct time table of Mediaeval services, with the help of such documentary and other evidence as may be forthcoming.

A complete table of all the times of ringing in Kincardineshire will be given later on, but here we may mention the following from elsewhere:—

Birse,	...	...	... 9	... 11		...	s. 12
Peterculter,	...	8	... 10			...	s. 12
Midmar,	...	8	... 10		... s. 11.30		
S. Andrews,	...	8² ...	9	... s. 11²			
Montrose,	...	8²	... s. 10²				s. 2
Stracathro,	...		... 10	... s. 11			
Skene,	... ...		... 10		... s. 11.30		
Ellon,	... ...				... s. 11.30	... s. 5.30	
„ (Com. Sundays)	...	9	... s. 11		... s. 5.30		
Stirling,	... ...	8		... s. 11¹ ...	s 2¹	... s. 6.30¹	
Roxburgh,	...	8					
Morebattle,	...	8					
Kilmore,	... ...	8 (formerly).					
Ratho,	... ...	8					
Braemar,	... ...	8					

Before the Reformation there were 5 bells at Dundee on which "six score and nine straiks" were given three times a day, to call to "matins, mess, and evensang."

Nothing has as yet been said about Evensong bells. These are very rare, and in country churches afternoon and evening services seem of modern introduction. In cases where the bell is rung twice beforehand, it seems to be a mere copy of what is done in the morning.

As might be expected from the long sway of Presbyterianism, the passing bell[2] is no longer rung, nor is there any ringing at burials beyond tolling the bell for a few minutes as the procession approaches the churchyard. In some parishes this is said to be rapidly dying out, being merely done at the request of very old people. Within living memory it was the custom to ring a hand bell in the procession,[3] but this has now completely died out. In 1643 the Town Council of Aberdeen forbade the use of bells at funerals as superstitious; its zeal, however, at that moment was probably stimulated by the near presence of a Covenanting Army.

Church bells are often rung on week days: in most cases this is for some purely utilitarian purpose, which now-a-days obscures any other significance the

---

[1] All simultaneously. [2] Tenor. "s." = "for service at."

[2] In the Burgh Recor ls of Dundee "it is statute that an ony person cause the gret bells to be rung for either saul mass or dirige, he sall pay forty pence to the Kirk werk."

"The bell is decernit till ring friely for all neighbours and comburgesses at ony neighbours decease without ony contribution, except twelve pence to the sacristan ringer of the bell alanerly." The fee was sometimes dispensed with as a mark of respect. *Old Dundee*, Alex. Maxwell, p. 42.

[3] Elgin Session Records, 23rd June, 1591. Quatsumevir persoun being diseasit within this burgh he seiknes departs this lyif on adverteising the minister, redar, or ane elder in their absens sall want the convey the faythfull to their buriall . . . and forbids the belman to knell the hand bell for thame or any other bell."

practice may once have had. Ringing as a fire alarm, on Sacramental Fast-days, and for Presbytery meetings,[1] &c., sufficiently explains itself, but some notice must be given to the ringing at different hours through the day. As this is now invariably a secular use, we shall consider it more fully when we have spoken of the connection of Church bells in Scotland with secular authority.

In the larger towns the steeples of the parish churches, together with their contents, are often the property of the municipality, and are considered to be "Town Steeples." In such cases the church is allowed the use of one or more of the bells on Sundays, but the town authorities have the control and maintenance of them, and use them as town bells during the week. The reason for this is not far to seek. In former times we again and again find a town acquiring a lien on the bells in exchange for helping to build the steeple, or undertaking to keep it in order.

The following extract from the Burgh Records[2] of Peebles exhibits a good instance of this:—

"1778, December 29. The Council, in conjunction with the heritors, agree to the proposition of building a new church, . . . The town to be at the expense of building the steeple and furnishing it with a clock and bells, for which it is to be the property of the burgh."

At Aberdeen the steeple, clock, and bells of the parish church of S. Nicholas are the property of the burgh authorities, who assume complete control over them. The same is the case at Dundee, Stirling, Forfar, and Montrose.

Hence we often find church bells used as town bells on week days for such purposes as ringing at meal hours, &c. In many cases, however, the town has a bell of its own hanging in a steeple quite unconnected with any church, sometimes standing by itself, and sometimes forming part of Town House or Tolbooth. In addition to that of S. Nicholas Church, Aberdeen has steeples on both Town House and Tolbooth, each with their bells.

Besides various meal hours through the day, 5 or 6 in the morning, and 8, 9 or 10 at night are the usual times for the ringing of town bells or their substitutes. The early morning ringing seems to be simply to call work people, but the evening bell may well be the survival of the Curfew.[3] In the latter part of the 17th century at Elgin both the great bell of St. Giles' and the Tolbooth bell were rung at 4 a.m. The Tolbooth bell at Aberdeen is now rung at 5 a.m. and 8 p.m., and also for meetings of the Town Council. The 10 p.m. bell remains in many places, among which are St. Andrews, Perth, Dundee, Montrose and Forfar.

Ellon supplies a good instance of the way in which the adaptation of an old custom to modern needs has obscured the purpose of its introduction. There the

---

[1] Perth Session Records, Oct. 6, 1578. "The session ordains James Sym uptaker of the casualities that intervenes in the kirk, to buy a tow to the litte skellit bell—the which bell shall only be rung to the affairs of the kirk, also to the examinations, or to the assemblies."

[2] Chambers' *History of Peebles*, p. 267.

[3] In Perth Burgh Records, 1657, is "An Act requiring obedience to the bell for putting out fires." Also in the Session Records, Feb. 6, 1586-7. "The session orlains Nicol Balmain to ring the Curfew and work-men's Bell in the morning, and evening, the space of ane quarter of an hour, at the times appointed, viz., four hours in the morning and eight at even."

church bell is rung at 8 p.m. in summer and 7 p.m. in winter, and this seems to be the remnant of the curfew. Now, however, it is looked upon as the signal for shutting the shops, and to such an extent, that since Wednesday became the "shopkeepers' half-holiday" it has been rung on that day at 2 p.m.

A few other uses will be noticed later.

Before closing this general sketch it will not be out of place to refer to several abuses connected with bells which are to be found in many places.

Too often country beadles indulge in what they are pleased to call "getting the double on the bell," i.e., swinging it to and fro like a factory bell. It is impossible to say too much against this practice, which has again and again resulted in the destruction of bells never meant to bear such usage. Very near akin to this is the all prevalent mania for wheels where the bells are too small for them, and also that other mania for a huge counterbalance, which in the case of large bells prevents their being properly used, and in that of small ones is, like the wheel, merely a contrivance for "getting the double" with a little less exertion on the part of the ringer. Where a large bell has been obtained from England, the local people often see fit to improve (?) the fittings of a good founder by the introduction of some questionable addition of their own.

In most of the smaller churches where the bells are hung in out of the way places, means of access are usually wanting, and so they cannot be properly kept in order. It is a common thing to have to send several miles before ladders of sufficient length can be found to reach them, and it is still more common to find the hangings in such an insecure condition as to render ringing absolutely dangerous. If there is a fine tower with a good staircase, what is lacking by nature is usually made up for by art in the shape of gross neglect, the belfry being given up to birds and bats. Disused bells are extremely common; in ruined churches where the bell remains, the slightest pretext is thought sufficient excuse for not ringing, and indeed, when once the rope is broken, it is the aim and object of every beadle to let the ivy grow over the belfry, and the birds build inside the bell. One can hardly do the authorities the injustice of supposing that such a state of things would be allowed to continue if they knew it.

This practical neglect of bells is nothing new,[1] as the following quotation will show.[2]

"Bells were not universal, even at the end of the last century. It often happened that where they were provided there was nowhere to hang them: a theologian of 1679 inveighs against 'that pitiful spectacle, bells hanging upon trees for want of bell-houses.' Such 'a bell tree' is still shown in the park at Auldbar;[3] but here, obviously, the bell was not placed on the church for the same reason that

---

[1] Nor has it been confined to Scotland, as may be seen by consulting Lukis or Ellacombe, who speak in no measured terms of the then state of not a few of the English belfries in the more remote districts. There has, however, been a great change for the better since interest in bells has been revived, and it is noteworthy that nowhere have belfry reforms been more in evidence than in those counties, of whose bells accounts have been published.

[2] *Scottish Abbeys and Cathedrals.* J. Robertson, p. 102.

[3] It is said to be gone now.

the campanile at the Curral in Madeira is built in the churchyard wall, and at the sequestered church of Ardclach in Murray on the neighbouring promontory—in order that the bell might be better heard—the church itself, in all these cases, lying in a deep ravine . . . . in the Statistical Account, published between 1791 and 1799. We read . . of two churches at Morven, in the West Highlands, which, without seats or bells, might as properly be called sheds, . . of St Mungo's, in Annandale, as 'having no bell . . .'"

We have seen the gradual development of the present form of bell and of existing customs and usages; also the position of Scotland in such matters considered in its relation to England and the Continent. We have in particular observed its close connection with the latter, as manifested by the amount of foreign work there is, and also by the Continental methods of ringing which prevail. We have noticed the effects which Scotch history and religious thought have had on bells in later times, and we have glanced at the state of things at the present day. So that having seen the importance of this branch of Ecclesiology, and as far as circumstances allow, obtained a clear idea of bells in Scotland generally, we are ready to consider the Church Bells of Kincardineshire.

II. ON THE CHURCH BELLS OF KINCARDINESHIRE.

There are 75 bells in Kincardineshire and they are distributed as follows :—
I. As regards possession.
All the bells attached to churches on ancient sites are now in the hands of the Established Church, which possesses several besides, making a total for that body of - - - - - - - - - - - - 32

The Episcopal Church has	12
„ Roman „	2
„ U. P. „	1
„ Free (and E. Coast)	14
In municipal possession	5
„ private „	9
	75

II. As regards age and kind.

Mediaeval	1
Dutch Renaissance	2
Scotch. { 18th century	4
{ Modern	13
Irish	1
English. { Early 18th century	1
{ Late „ (?)	1
{ Modern	34
Modern (?) Foreign (Ships' bells)	2
Doubtful. { Ancient (?)	4
{ Modern (?)	12
	75

III. As regards "collections."

"Collections" of 3	1
„ 2	2
Single bells	71
	75

The "collection" of 3 is at St. Cyrus, and consists of a ringing bell and two disused "dead" clock bells; the collections of 2 are at S. James's (Ep. Ch.), Stonehaven, and the Town Steeple, Stonehaven. The former consists of a ringing bell and an old disused ship's bell, and the latter of two ringing bells, of which one is disused.

In 1505 Sir Robert Arbuthnott put two bells in the belfry he built at the west end of Arbuthnott Church. He also built a similar belfry at the north west corner of the Arbuthnott Chapel, and it is extremely probable that he put two bells there as well, because two rope holes still remain in the floor.

There is but one bell now in the county which can with any degree of certainty be called a Mediaeval. That is the old bell at Strachan, which probably belongs either to the end of the Fifteenth or the beginning of the Sixteenth century. It is very small (13¾ in.) with a long waist, rounded shoulders and no crown. Although the surface is rough and the single bead above the soundbow irregular, yet the general outline and proportions, the finish of the inside and the carefully moulded canons seem to indicate that it is the work of a regular bell founder and no mere local effort. The canons are most peculiar; they are not at right angles to one another, nor yet parallel in pairs, and they seem to have had a sort of beading on them.

The origin of such a bell as this is a difficult matter to determine, as the small amount of evidence is very conflicting. The general outline of the bell is decidedly foreign, but the canons are smaller in proportion than is usual in foreign work; the rough surface and lack of ornament seem to suggest a different origin. It is rather like the 17th at Perth—a fine "AVE" bell of the Fourteenth century, probably foreign. This bell also has a single bead above the soundbow, and very rounded shoulders, but it has an elaborate inscription and a much longer waist.

The best explanation seems to be that the bell at Strachan is the work of one of those itinerant founders who were common in former times when means of transit were not so good as they are now. This would at once account for the good shape and canons, and also for the absence of inscription or decorations, as itinerants were usually capable men, though they often did not carry more than the appliances necessary for work of the plainest order.

The following story is told in Strachan with reference to the bell:—A long while ago, two bells were cast at the same time, one being much better than the other. The better of the two was intended for Strachan, the other being for Birse. When they were being taken up the Dee valley in the same cart the inferior bell was accidentally (?) left at Strachan, while the other was taken on to Birse and afterwards became famous for its clear tone, giving rise to the local saying, "as clear as the bell o' Birse." So that Birse has all along had the credit for what really belonged to Strachan! If there is anything in this story, which is very doubtful, it must refer to an older bell than that now at Birse, which was recast in 1813 from one dated 1675.

As mentioned above there were till lately two Mediaevals at Arbuthnott, one of which is said to have been taken to Montrose Rope Works. Whether this is true or not seems to be doubtful, as the bell now at the Rope Works is very small, uninscribed, without canons, and short in the waist—in fact it is suspiciously like a ship's bell. There also seem to have been Mediaevals at Maryculter and Marykirk till recently.

BELFRY AT NIGG.

BELFRY AT FETTERESSO.

OLD BELL AT STRACHAN.

LETTERING AND ORNAMENTS AT PORTLETHEN.

There is a very peculiar little bell at Brotherton House; it is known to be not modern, and it is said that the old bell of Benholm Church was taken to Brotherton at the revolution. It is 9⅝ in. in diameter, very long-waisted, and has two large canons on a very flat crown. There are two clear and regular beads above the soundbow, but otherwise the bell is quite plain. It is just possible that it may be 16th century work, although it is probably later.

Until 1869 there was a bell at Banchory Devenic inscribed :—

H. B. . ALLEINE . GOT . IN . DER . HOGE . SEI . ERE . 1597

As described by those who remember it, it was very long waisted, had four large canons at right angles to each other, and was about 18 in. in diameter. The inscription was in plain Roman capitals between two beads above the soundbow: on one side of the waist there was a "large scroll-like ornament," but otherwise the bell was perfectly plain. Is it possible that this ornament was Burgerhuys's phoenix, "HB." standing for H. Burgerhuys?

There are two Seventeenth century Dutch bells in the county—the older bell at Banchory Ternan, 1664, and that at Kinneff, 1679, both by Peter Ostens of Rotterdam. They are excellent examples of Dutch Renaissance work, and have fairly long waists, large canons, moulded crowns, thin and rather angular soundbows, and bands of mouldings instead of the simple English beads. They both have a border of large strawberry leaves below the inscription, and an elaborate ornamental band above. There is a small floral ornament at the beginning of each inscription, and a figure of a recumbent ox between the founders' names: this seems to be Ostens' foundry mark. The Kinneff bell is 23 in. in diameter, being 4½ in. larger than that at Banchory, and has the inscription in Dutch instead of Latin like the latter: the tone, moreover, is much finer. The ornamental band above the inscription consists of angels ringing hand bells amidst elaborate conventional foliage; it is more than twice as broad as that at Banchory, which consists of figures[1] reclining amidst grapes, flowers and leaves, and is much more delicate than the one at Kinneff. The canons at Banchory are slightly ornamented. The clappers in both cases are the originals and are very much worn; they seem to have represented twisted cords with tassels.

Other bells by the same founder are the 4th at Montrose, 1675—perhaps the most profusely ornamented bell in this part of the country—and, until it was recast in 1818, a bell at Alloa, 1668.

Here must be noticed the bells of Mains of Barras, Dunnottar House, and Ecclesgreig House: also the old bell at Blairs. These are all small, plain, long-waisted bells without inscriptions. They all seem to be prior to the last century and may be very old. That at Barras seems to be of Seventeenth century date, and that at Dunnottar possibly much earlier.

Of Eighteenth century Scotch work there are only four examples now hanging in the county, and they are all from the Old Aberdeen foundry. There is, however, another one which has been recast with the old inscription reproduced.

---

[1] It is often very hard to say whether these Renaissance figures are intended for angels or cupids, as the revived paganism made the representations very similar. In the case of the Banchory bell they are probably cupids, being wingless and amidst bacchanalian surroundings, but at Kinneff they seem to be angels, as they are winged and are ringing bells.

The history of this Old Aberdeen foundry has not as yet been thoroughly investigated, but there is sufficient material to enable us to construct an imperfect record of it, of which only an outline will be given here, fuller treatment being reserved for "Church Bells of Aberdeenshire," to which it by right belongs.

It is impossible at present to say when the Aberdeen foundry was started. As yet, however, no Aberdeen bell has been found earlier than that at Cushnie, 1686, by Patrick Kilgour, who cast a bell for Aberdeen Cathedral in 1688, having been admitted to the Guild of Hammermen as a wheelwright in 1662. According to the Burgess Roll of Aberdeen, one Patrick Kilgoure or Killgower, a watchmaker at Old Aberdeen, applied for and received rights of freedom in the New Town, and was obliged "not to . . . . work in . . . any of the trads . . . only that it shall be leasome to him to make or mend watches or cast bells as he may have occasion." There is none of his work in Kincardineshire, but his successor, Albert Gely, whose foundry was at the head of Baillie Forsyth's Close, is represented at Portlethen, 1702. This is a pretty little bell on a good Low Country model, with neatly cast letters and mouldings. Above and below the inscription it has a peculiar kind of ornamental border, of which isolated pieces are used as stops between the words. A sheaf of corn, placed horizontally, seems to be the founder's mark. Douglas speaks of him as having "refounded most of the bells in" Aberdeen, and several yet remain in that county. He it was who offered to recast the King's College bells if the authorities would allow him a third of the metal. His latest date found as yet is 1713.

His successor was John Mowat, called a "blacksmith" in old records, admitted to the Guild of Hammermen in 1717, and made Burgess of Guild in 1719. He seems to have done a large business as locksmith, clockmaker, and general blacksmith, in addition to casting bells, indeed several of his clocks are still in existence. He "demitted his office of Deaconry" of the Hammermen in 1725, was master from 1730 to 1733, master and boxmaster from 1738 to 1743, and master again from 1744 to 1746. During the next few years he became involved in reference to some guild money, and he does not seem to have come out with very clean hands. His bells are very numerous, especially in Aberdeenshire. He died in 1771.

Kincardineshire now possesses three bells by him, viz., those at Nigg, 1759, Durris, 1765, and Arbuthnott, 1736 (recast). There were formerly two others—one at Cookney, which came from S. Clements, Aberdeen, and the other at Drumlithic Town Steeple. Mowat, in common with the other Old Aberdeen founders, followed the Low Country model, but his bells have not such a good outline as Gely's, and have very clumsy shoulders. Mowat's tone was almost always "stony." He was profuse with decorations and used good clear letters, but he arranged them with such clumsiness and irregularity that his bells always have an inelegant and overloaded appearance. The ornaments on his earlier bells are bad copies of those of Ostens of Rotterdam, pieces of whose elegant friezes he used to fill up spaces, heedless of where the design began and ended. He even used Ostens' foundry mark, and put scraps of his flowers as stops between the words. His later bells are rather plainer and had a simple acanthus leaf frieze in place of Ostens' elaborate ornaments. Nearly all of them have a row of fleur-de-lys round the shoulder. Arbuthnott had one of the earlier

DUNNOTTAR.

NIGG.

SKENE ABERDEENSHIRE

bells and the Arbuthnott arms were on its waist. It was broken by falling during the fire of 1890, and was recast by Gillet & Johnston of Croydon, who reproduced in facsimile the inscriptions and decorations on what is otherwise a bell of their own model. The bell at Skene, however, cast in the previous year, shows us exactly what it was like. Nigg has one of the later kind—1759—and Durris has the latest of his found as yet. It was cast in 1765, and is without the border of fleur-de-lys round the shoulder.

"Andrew Lawson, Blacksmith," was admitted into the Burgess Guild of Old Aberdeen and also into the incorporation of Hammermen in 1765, and was deacon of the latter in 1773. He was Mowat's apprentice, and certainly succeeded to his bell foundry, as he used his models, lettering, and fleur-de-lys. He cast the bell of Dunnottar in 1783, and, as far as is known, this is the last of the bells from the Aberdeen foundry. It is exactly like one of Mowat's, but there is only one line of inscription, in which groups of Mowat's fleur-de-lys are inserted at intervals: there are no ornamental bands, but there is a space for a second line of inscription, all the beads and mouldings being identical with Mowat's. Lawson died in 1810. His son, also named Andrew, joined the Hammermen in 1793.

It has been thought right to detail the work of the Aberdeen foundry thus fully because of the extremely important position which it occupies. Insignificant though they are, those few fleur-de-lys, used on the Dunnottar bell, are perhaps one of the very latest survivals of the Ecclesiastical art of the middle ages. This is perfectly possible, because founders' stamps were handed on from one founder to another, and in England there are several cases of the use of Mediaeval stamps at the end of the 17th century. Moreover, in the foreign mouldings and outline of the Dunnottar bell we see a lingering survival of that Continental influence, which ever since the English wars in the 14th century had held such sway in Scotland.

There was a small foundry at Montrose in the early part of the present century, carried on first by David Barclay, and after 1820, by J. Dickson & Co., who are said to have done a large trade as general founders. The former cast the bell of Benholm in 1820, and the latter those of Fettercairn and Johnshaven. The Fettercairn bell is like an inverted basin, and is not quite circular. It has a row of large clear acanthus leaves above the soundbow. The Johnshaven bell is inscribed:—

MONTROSE
FOUNDRY   and is very much like a large ship's bell.
1828

The buildings where the foundry was carried on are still in existence on the West side of River Street. They are now occupied by Messrs. J. R. Mitchell & Co., who do not, however, cast bells.

Bells at Nigg (Est. Ch.), 1833, Cults, 1883, Cove, (E.C. Mission), 1887, Torry Free Church, 1890, and Drumtochty Castle, are by John Blaikie & Sons of Aberdeen, brass and general founders, who have been in existence about a century. The Nigg bell is one of their earliest. This is the firm who bought up all the old metal from S. Nicholas, Aberdeen, after the fire of 1874.

Banchory Devenic Free Church has a flower-pot bell cast by Simpson & Co., Ironfounders, of Footdee, Aberdeen, in 1861. This was the first and only bell they cast.

Marykirk Free Church disputes with Fettercairn the unenviable distinction of being the possessor of the worst bell in the county. This remarkable production is the work of John Duffus & Co. of Aberdeen, and enjoys the further distinction of being a "pre-disruption Free Church bell," having been cast in 1830.

The bell in the Town Steeple of New Stonehaven is by John C. Wilson & Co. of Glasgow; it is 35¼ in. in diameter, weighs 8 cwt., and is the largest and heaviest bell in the county. The annexed block[1] shows the shape of the bell and the method of hanging.

The bell of Drumlithie Town Steeple was recast from one of Mowat's by some Dundee founders in 1868.

There is a bell at Blairs College by J. Murphy of Dublin. It was cast in 1859, is 20 in. in diameter, has a flat crown, sharp shoulders and large canons decorated with a reed ornament. The tone is very good, and the clapper of unusual size.

We now come to the English bells.

At Fetteresso there is a bell inscribed:—

FETTERESSO J736

It is of good proportions and more than average tone; the form of the letters and the date point almost without doubt to Richard Phelps of Whitechapel as the founder.

The old bell of Maryculter (Est. Ch.) seems to be an English bell of a very third rate order, although it may be a Scotch "copy." The inscription runs:—

1786   1787

Of modern English bells there are 34. As the foundries are all in working, it will be as well to arrange them in the alphabetical order of the localities.

CROYDON.

Gillett & Johnston of Croydon recast the bell of Arbuthnott in 1890.

LONDON : *Clerkenwell.*

Bowen & Co. of Clerkenwell cast a 19 in. bell for the Established Church at Strachan in 1890.

LONDON : *Spitalfields.*

Drumlithie Free Church, 1858, Bieldside (Ep. Ch.), 1880, Banchory Ternan Free Church (28 in.), 1883, Cove (Ep. Ch.), 1887, and the Chapel in Craiginches Prison, 1890, have bells cast by John Warner & Sons of the Crescent Foundry.

LONDON : *Whitechapel.*

Besides the doubtful one mentioned above, Kincardineshire has 21 bells from this foundry. A bell at Glenbervie dated 1789[2] is from W. & T. Mears, and so was the old bell of St. Cyrus. Those of Bervie, 1791, Bervie Town, 1792,[2] and the Town Steeple, Stonehaven, 1793 are by Thomas Mears the elder. From Thomas Mears

---

[1] Kindly lent by Messrs. J. C. Wilson & Co.
[2] Almost certainly from this foundry, though without other inscription than the date.

BELLS OF KINCARDINESHIRE.

the younger we have the bells of Laurencekirk (Ep. Ch.), 1813, Mains of Davo, 1815,[2] Banchory Ternan (Est. Ch., 1820 '29 in.), Mains of Arbuthnott, 1823 (26¼ in.), Marykirk, 1826, Garvoc,[2] 1830, Fetteresso (Est. Ch.), 1834 (30½ in.), Drumlithie (Ep. Ch.), 1834,[2] and Fordoun, 1835[3] (34½ in.), the largest but one in the county. C. & G. Mears cast the 3 at St. Cyrus in 1845, 1846, and 1847 respectively; also the the bell at Fasque (Ep. Ch.) in 1846, and that of Catterline (Ep. Ch.) in 1849, which has a long inscription in Lombardic letters. Mears & Stainbank have cast bells for Lauriston Castle 1869, Cults Free Church, 1872, and Maryculter (Est. Ch.), 1896.

LOUGHBOROUGH.

Five bells are from J. Taylor & Co. of Loughborough: they are those of Banchory Devenic, recast 1869, Thornton Castle, 1879, Bourtreebush Free Church, 1884, Drumtochty (Ep. Ch.), 1885, and Cookney (25¼ in.), 1886.

SHEFFIELD.

Laurencekirk has a 24 in. "Steel bell" by Vickers Sons & Co. of Sheffield, 1895.

The illustration[4] shows a bell exactly like it with similar hangings.

The bells of Muchalls (Ep. Ch.), Cowie Mission Church and Durris Free Church also the 1st at St. James's (Ep. Ch.), Stonehaven, are old ship's bells; the first mentioned was fished up out of the sea by some Cowie line fishers, and is a modern bell without interest.

That of Durris Free Church has elaborate ornamental borders and seems to be a last century Low Country bell. The 1st at S. James's, Stonehaven is of interest because it bears some resemblance to Danckwart's bell at Stirling.[1]

Of unknown origin are the bells of Banchory Ternan (Ep. Ch.), and Kinneff Free Church, both 1851; also the uninscribed bells of Rickarton, q.s., and of S. Cyrus and Johnshaven Free Churches.

[1] v. p. 7.
[2] Almost certainly from this foundry, though without other inscription than the date.
[3] v. Appendix.
[4] Kindly lent by Messrs. Vickers Sons & Co.

The bells of Luthermuir U.P. Church, of Maryculter and Strachan Free Churches, and of several schools, etc., are diminutive and entirely without interest.

Arbuthnott (Ep. Ch.), Durris (Ep. Ch.) and Stonehaven (R.C. Ch.) are without bells. So also are two modern Established Chapels, two U.P. and five Free Churches ; also the " Berean " Conventicle at Sauchieburn.

The following bells are disused :—Nigg (Old); Banchory Ternan (Old); the 1st and 2nd of St. Cyrus; the 1st of S. James's, Stonehaven; the 1st at the Town Steeple of Stonehaven ; the Town bell of Bervie, and the bell at Mains of Barras.

The following ancient bells not in use are carefully preserved as objects of historic interest :—

Strachan—In the Session House adjoining the (Est.) Church.
Maryculter—In the Church Hall adjoining the (Est.) Church.

There is comparatively little worthy of note in the way of ringing customs in Kincardineshire beyond the early bells at the Parish Churches.

The hours at which these are rung are shown in the subjoined table :—

Parish.	Time of Ringing.			Time of Service.	
Fordoun	8	10		11	
Garvoc	8	10		11	
Laurencekirk	8 (discontinued)	10		11	
Banchory Ternan	8	10			11.30
Maryculter	8	10 (discontinued ; 10.45 a.m. substituted)			12
Glenbervie		10		11	
St. Cyrus	? 8 (discontinued)	10		11	
Durris		10	(discontinued ; 11 a.m. substituted in 1884).		12
Marykirk	9 (discontinued)	10		11	
Bervie	9		10.30 (discontinued) in 1872.	12 (discontinued ; 11 a.m. substituted 1872)	
Arbuthnott	9			11.30	
Fetteresso	9			11.30	
Dunnottar	9 (discontinued)			11	11.30
Kinneff				11	11.30
Banchory Devenic				11	12
Nigg				11	12
Benholm	? 9 (discontinued)	10.30		11	
Strachan		10.30			11.30
Fettercairn	NO RINGING (except for service)			11	

For the significance of the above, readers may refer to the remarks on this part of the subject in the general introduction.

The 10 o'clock bell at Cookney *quoad sacra* Established Church seems to be a survival of the Scripture reading mentioned on p. 8.

The following table shows the times of ringing of the town bells at Drumlithie and Stonehaven:—

	WEEKDAYS.					SUNDAYS.	
	A.M.			P.M.		A.M.	P.M.
Drumlithie	6	9	...	...	10		
Stonehaven		9	2	8	9[1]		...
				[1] (discontinued)			
Stonehaven (New) 5.30 (discontinued)	...	9	2	8	...	11	5.30

The bell of the chapel at Johnshaven used to be rung daily at 6 a.m. and 8 p.m. It was also rung to warn ships in foggy weather.

In the last century a custom was instituted in some of the Deeside churches of ringing the bell at 12 on Saturday night to warn the salmon fishers that it was time to stop work, and also at 12 on Sunday night to let them know that they might resume. But this has not been done for many years.

Occasionally it will be found that Free Churches ring an hour or half an hour before service in addition to ringing-in. This is sometimes to give extra notice, sometimes for Sunday school, and occasionally a mere copy of what is done at the Established Church.

DESCRIPTION OF BELLS.

ARBUTHNOTT.   S. Ternan.   I.

on crown   1221

IOA | MOWAT | ME | FECIT | VET | ABD | 1736 | IN | USUM | ECCLESIÆ | DE: ARBUTHNOT | SABBATA | PANGO | FUNERA | PLANGO §......... ....§

on waist   A

above soundbow   **RECAST BY GILLETT & Co CROYDON 1890.**

A.........Panel with Arbuthnott arms.	20¼"
§.........§ Ornamental band.	1 Cwt. 2 qr.
| Floral stop.	Old bell :—
‡ ,, ,, blundered.	
	1 Cwt. 1 qr.

Ornaments from Ostens of Rotterdam. Broken in fire of 1890; recast[1] with inscription, decorations, etc., in facsimile. Denison headed.

In 16th cent. turret at W. end of Nave.

9 a.m., s. 11.30 a.m.

[1] The bell at Skene, Aberdeenshire, is exactly like what this was before being recast; its note is F♯ and the tone is stony.

The following shows that there were formerly two bells where this one is :—

"[Robertus Arbuthnotus] Primum enim eam Templi Arbuthnotici partem quae occidentem spectat, elegantiore quam prius erat opere extruendam, ac rotundam turrim suspendendis campanis idoneam ei parti superimposuit, eandemque duabus campanis ornavit."—"*Originis et Incrementi Arbuthnoticae Familiae Descriptio Historica, etc.* Auctore, D. A. Arbuthnoto."

This is said to have been in 1505. It is probable that the existing bell contains the metal of these.

There is a similar turret at the north west corner of the Arbuthnott Chapel, which we are told in the document quoted above was also built by Sir Robert Arbuthnott.[1] It is therefore highly probable that he put two bells there also, and this is confirmed by the fact that two rope holes still remain in the floor. The bell in the works of the Montrose Rope and Sail Co. is said to have been brought from here: it is uninscribed, is 11½ in. in diameter, not long in the waist, and without canons—in fact, suspiciously like an old ship's bell.

[1] Deinde fanum quoddam egregie et artis et materiae qualitate lapide ad templi angulum qui Eurum spectat a solo erexit . . . . . . Insulam Arbuthnoticam nunc vocant . . . . .

Chapel of S. Mary.   **PEATTIE.**
NO BELL.

Episcopal Church of S. Mary.   **PARKNOOK.**
NO BELL.

Mains of Arbuthnott.   I.

T. MEARS OF LONDON FECIT 1823.   )◯⦿◯(..........

26½"

In clock tower of farm buildings, d. 1792. Used as a clock bell, but seldom rung.

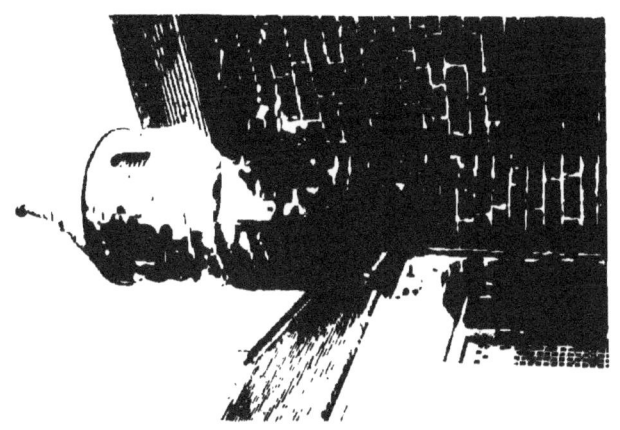
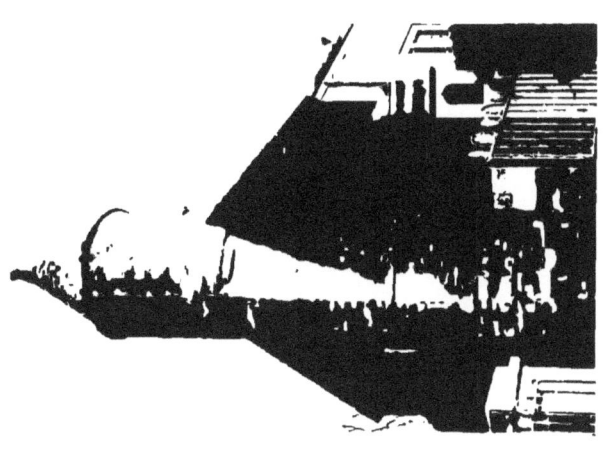

BELL TURRETS AT ARBUTHNOTT.

BANCHORY DEVENIC. S. Devenic. 1.
J. TAYLOR & CO. LOUGHBOROUGH 1869.

on waist

1597. RECAST 1859.

18¾
1 cwt. 1 qr. 22 lbs.

In bird-cage belfry over W. end.
11 a.m. s. 12.
Was recast from old bell inscribed :—

H B . . ALLEINE . GOT . IN . DER . HOGE . SEI . ERE . 1597

probably about 17¼"
1 cwt. 6 lbs.

The statement in the new Statistical Account, p. 185, that this bell was cast at Gotin obviously arises from a misreading of the inscription. Cf. bell at Comrie, 1583.

Chapel of S. Ternan.   FINDON.
NO BELL.
Site doubtful.

Episcopal Church of S. Andrew.   BIELDSIDE. 1.

on soundbow

J. WARNER & SONS LONDON 1880

In belfry over W. end.

12"
1 qr. 16 lbs.

Ch. formerly stood in the part of the parish near Mannofield; moved here in 1895, where it is now in a part of Peterculter that was formerly in Banchory Devenic.

"Quoad Sacra" Established Ch.   PORTLETHEN. 1.

‡ MR ALEXANDER · THOMSON ⁑ ALBERTVS   OELY   ME   FECIT ABD   ANNO DOM ‡ MDCCII

§ Founder's mark.
‖ Ornamental stop.
†   ,,   ,, blundered.

13⅜"

Broken mouthed ; in bird cage belfry over W. end. Erroneously said to be an old ship's bell—a common coast-side tradition, Cf. Nigg.

"Quoad Sacra" Established Ch.   CULTS. 1.

⊥ I AM A CHIP OF OLD LAWRIE ✠ J BLAIKIE & SONS

on waist   1883

13⅞"

No canons ; in wooden belfry over E. end.
Cast by John Blaikie & Sons of Aberdeen from a piece of the old tenor of S. Nicholas, Aberdeen, nicknamed "Old Lawrie" on account of its dedication to S. Lawrence.

BELLS OF KINCARDINESHIRE.

Free Ch. 1.

on waist

**PRESENTED
TO THE FREE CHURCH
OF BANCHORY DEVENICK
BY THE BROTHERS AND SISTERS
NEPHEWS & NIECES
OF MRS THOMPSON OF BANCHORY
SEPTEMBER
1861**

20⅞"

A canonless flower-pot-shaped bell by Simpson & Co. of Aberdeen.

Free Ch. CULTS. 1.

MEARS & STAINBANK FOUNDERS LONDON, 1872.

25⅝"
3 cwt. 2 qrs. 18 lbs.

Note.—Although the *Quoad Sacra* Established Church at Mannofield is partly in this parish, the tower and bell are in Aberdeenshire.

BANCHORY TERNAN. S. Ternan. 1.

§ SOLI DEO GLORIA · PETERVS † OSTENS ROTERODAMI ME FECIT · A°. 1 6 6 4

§ Detached floral ornament ; a small rose and leaves.
† Figure of a recumbent ox.

18¼"

In small bird-cage belfry on south side of circular watch house in old churchyard. Disused.

Established Ch. 1.

T MEARS OF LONDON FECIT 1820 ○○○·········

29"

In tower at S. end.
8 a.m., 10 a.m., s. 11.30.

? Chapel of S. Mary. MARYFIELD.
NO BELL.
Site doubtful.

Episcopal Church of S. Ternan.

at top of waist ✠ A.D. ✠
    1 8 5 1

15½"

A canonless flower-pot-shaped bell in arch belfry over W. end.

Free Ch. 1.

CAST BY JOHN WARNER & SONS LONDON 1888.

28"
5 cwt.

Fixed "dead" on a beam built into walls of tower at S. E. corner. The clapper is moved by a rope tied to a piece of iron fixed at right angles to it!

BENHOLM.   S. Marnan.   1.

DAVID BARCLAY MONTROSE 1820

18"

In bird cage belfry over E. end.
10.30 a.m. [? formerly also at 9 a.m.] s. 11 a.m.
There is a tradition that the bell from this church was taken away to Brotherton at the revolution, together with the Church Plate.

Established Chapel.   JOHNSHAVEN.   1.
on waist   MONTROSE
              FOUNDRY   15¼"
              1825

Hemispherical crown, long waist and large soundbow; no canons. Rung at 5 p.m., s. 5.30 p.m; formerly also in fogs, and if a vessel came ashore; until c. 1880 also at 6 a.m., and 8 p.m. daily, exc. Suns.

Free Ch.   JOHNSHAVEN.   1.
NO INSCRIPTION.

14¼"

Without canons; said to have been brought from St. Petersburg by a Captain Mearns.

Brotherton House.
NO INSCRIPTION.

9⅞"

A peculiar bell with a long waist and two large canons: very smooth and new looking, but said to be very old. May possibly be of late 16th or early 17th century date.

CATTERLINE.   S. Catharine.

Parish now united to KINNEFF.

NO BELL.
Hardly anything left except the churchyard.

Episcopal Church of S. Philip.   1.

on waist   ḦOG OPUS INSPIGIṮO IESU VINGUSE ḦRUEGO
             EX DONO GULIELMI ET JOSEPHI HASKOLL
             HNNO SHLUTIS MDCCCXLIX

on soundbow   MEARS LONDINI

21"

In arch belfry over W. end.

DUNNOTTAR.   S. Bridget.   1.

TO DINOTER ††††† AND^W. LAWSON OLD ABD 1783 †††††††

† fleur-de-lys.

18"

Some of the canons broken; fleur-de-lys ornament much corroded in parts. Exactly like one of Mowat's bells. So far as is known, the latest of the Old Aberdeen bells.

In bird cage belfry over W. end.

11 a.m., s. 11.30 a.m., 6 p.m.

Chapel of S. Bridget in DUNNOTTAR CASTLE.
The Parish Church until 1394.

NO BELL.

On the west gable is still left the stone cill of what seems to have been a bird cage belfry of much the usual type.

The two bells now in use at the castle gate are diminutive, modern, and without interest.

Chapel of S. Ninian.	DUNNOTTAR.

NO BELL.

Remains of chapel buried under one of the gardens of Dunnottar House.

Chapel of S.	? URAS.

NO BELL.
Site doubtful.

Episcopal Church of S. James.	STONEHAVEN. 2.

(1) *NO INSCRIPTION.*

abt. 13″

(2) said to be :—B 1800

abt. 18″

No. 1 is lying rusty and disused in the base of the campanile above the door into the vestry. It belonged to a Norwegian vessel that was wrecked off Cowie, and was the bell of the new church before the 2nd was brought from the old. It has two ornamental bands and no canons.

No. 2 is hung at the top of the campanile without means of access; it was the bell of the old church. Perhaps "B" stands for "Barclay" of Montrose.

Roman Catholic Church of Our Lady of the Immaculate Conception.	STONEHAVEN.

NO BELL.

Established Chapel of S. Bridget.	STONEHAVEN.

NO BELL.

Dunnottar House.	1.

NO INSCRIPTION.

10⅝″

Without canons but may be very old: possibly from the old chapel of S. Ninian.

Town Steeple.	STONEHAVEN. 2.

(1) *NO INSCRIPTION.*

17½″

(2) 1 7 9 3 ◊◯◊ ....

22″

No. 1 is disused.
No. 2, probably by T. Mears of London, has some of the canons broken.
Rung daily at 9 a.m., 2 p.m. and 8 p.m. ; formerly also at 9 p.m.

Hung between beams at base of spire.

Mains of Barras. 1.
NO INSCRIPTION.

8"

Before the old house of Barras was pulled down the bell used to hang in a small bird cage belfry which is still preserved, but whether it was the alarm bell of the house or a bell from any old chapel it is impossible to say, as it is very small and has been painted. It seems to have canons, and certainly is not modern, but its age is doubtful. It is now hung in an iron bracket outside W. gable of farm house, where it was put in 1863 by request of the Governors of Donaldson's Hospital, Edinburgh.

DURRIS.   S. Congal. 1.

IOHN · MOWAT OLD · ABD FE 1765 IN usuM ECCLESLE DE
DURRES SABATA PANGO FUNERA · PLANGO ✢ ✢ ✢ ....
✝ ✝ ✝........
✝ ✝ ✝........ Ornamental border.   16¾"
✢ ✢ ✢..........same inverted.

One of the latest of Mowat's bells. His usual fleur-de-lys border above inscription is absent, and lines of inscription are further apart than usual.
In small bird-cage belfry over W. end, which has been covered by an erection of wood. 11 a.m., s. 12. Prior to 1884 at 10 a.m instead of 11 a.m.

Episcopal Church (private).
NO BELL.

Free Ch. 1.
on waist   F O R T U N E

12"

An old ship's bell.
No canons ; good but irregular ornamental border on soundbow, and a double one on shoulder. Probably from an old Low Country or Baltic vessel. Perhaps 18th century work.
In a sort of closed bird-cage belfry over E. end, and inaccessible.

FETTERCAIRN.   S. Mark. 1.

on waist   **J · DICKSON & C·**
                  MONTROSE
                    1821

above soundbow   *   *   *   *........ ....

22¼" - 22¼"
height 15½"
C♯

* Acanthus leaf

Hemispherical crown apparently mutilated; extremely short waist. A kind of inverted metal basin. A row of very clear acanthus leaves just above soundbow.

In small tower below spire at W. end.
No ringing except for service [at 11 a.m.]
The previous bell used to hang in a tree on a hill called the "bell hillock."

Chapel of S. Adamnan (?)	**ARNHALL**	
NO BELL.		

Site doubtful.

Episcopal Church of S. Andrew.	**FASQUE.**	1.

C & G MEARS FOUNDERS LONDON 1846

14"

In arch belfry over W. end.

FETTERESSO. S. Caran. 1.

FETTERESSO J736

19¼"

Of good proportions and more than average tone; probably by Richard Phelps of Whitechapel.
Said to be occasionally rung at funerals.
Church in ruins.

Established Ch.		1.

THOMAS MEARS OF LONDON FOUNDER 1834

30½"

D

In town at S. end.
9 a.m., s. 11.30 a.m., and 6 p.m.

Chapel of S. S. Mary & Nathalan.	**COWIE.**	
NO BELL.		

In ruins.

Chapel of S.	? **ELSICK.**	
NO BELL.		

Churchyard only.

Episcopal Church of S. Ternan.	**MUCHALLS.**	1.
NO INSCRIPTION.		

12½"

A canonless ship's bell fished up from the sea by some Cowie line fishers in 1847; formerly hung in the old belfry, but now in wooden frame on N. side of chancel, awaiting hanging in new arch belfry over W. end.

Episcopal Mission Room.	**COWIE.**	1.

An old ship's bell without interest.

Episcopal Chapel of S. Mary within COWIE HOUSE.

Sanctus bell :

on crown + SIT NOMEN DOMINI BENEDICTVM

on waist LAVRENS ECCE VOCOR

MEARS ET STAINBANK LOND. ME FECERVNT
EX CAMPANA ECCL. S. NICOL. ABRED.
QVÆ FVSA MCCCLI
REFVSA MDCXXXIV
FRACTA EST MDCCCLXXIV.

on soundbow ....CAP. S. MARIÆ DE COWIE MDCCCXCVI.

6½"
F♯

A plain hand bell with polished surface and of fine clear tone. Inscription incised; part withheld by special request.

"Quoad Sacra" Established Ch.   COOKNEY.   1.

J ✦ TAYLOR & Cº FOUNDERS LOUGHBOROUGH 1886 ✦

25⅛"
3 cwt. 2 qrs. 25 lbs.

In large arch belfry over W. end. Rung by rope in N. W. corner running over series of pulleys up inside gable to roof ridge whence goes a chain to an iron lever fastened to the wheel, "because it was too stiff to ring as it was." When the church was rebuilt in 1885 the old bell was taken away, and after passing through several hands was at length bought by Messrs. John Blaikie & Sons of Aberdeen, who melted it. It seems to have been one of Mowat's, cast about the middle of the last century, with a fleur-de-lys border and the inscription in two lines. Originally cast for S. Clement's, Aberdeen, it was sent to Cookney on the purchase of a new bell for the former.

"Quoad Sacra" Established Ch.   RICKARTON.   1.
NO INSCRIPTION.

18"

Obtained 1871. No canons.
In arch belfry over N. end.

Established Chapel of S. John.   STONEHAVEN.
NO BELL.

Free Ch.   BOURTREEBUSH. 1.

on waist I: GAVION AND Cº FOUNDERS.
TO THE FREE CHURCH OF SCOTLAND, BOURTREEBUSH.
FROM ROBERT AND HELEN GRANT LUMSDEN
MDCCCLXXXIV.

13¾"
2 qr. 10 lbs.

In small bird-cage belfry over E. end.

New Town Steeple. STONEHAVEN. 1.

JOHNC. WILSON FOUNDER GLASGOW. No. 580

on waist SPIRE, CLOCK & BELL ERECTED BY THE TOWN COUNCIL
OF THE NEWTOWN OF STONEHAVEN BY SUBSCRIPTION 1857.

35¼"
8 cwt.

G♯

9 a.m., 2 p.m., 8 p.m.; formerly also 5.30 a.m.
Sundays: 11 a.m., 5.30 p.m., "as slowly as possible."
On special occasions, etc., every 15 minutes from 12 to 2 p.m.

FORDOUN. S. Palladius. 1.

THOMAS MEARS OF LONDON FOUNDER 1835.

34½"

The largest but one in the county.
In tower at W. end.
8 a.m., 10 a.m.; s. 11 a.m. Also at 5 and 6 p.m. when there is service at 6.

Chapel of S. Palladius IN THE CHURCHYARD.
NO BELL.

Chapel of S. Catharine KINCARDINE.
NO BELL.
Churchyard only.

Chapel of S. ? TEMPLE.
NO BELL.
Site doubtful.

Episcopal Church of S. Palladius DRUMTOCHTY. 1.

J: TAYLOR AND C⁰ LOUGHBOROUGH.

21¾"
1 cwt. 3 qr. 11 lbs.

Cast in 1885.
At top of campanile between chancel and S. transept.

Drumtochty Castle.

A small bell without interest recently recast by J. Blaikie & Sons of Aberdeen from an uninscribed bell not more than a century old.

GARVOC. S. James [the Great.] 1.

1 8 3 0

18¼"

By T. Mears of London. Brought from Laurencekirk in 1896.
In very fine bird-cage belfry over W. end.
8 a.m. [10 a.m. also, until 1891] s. 11 a.m.

Old bell:—
NO INSCRIPTION.

18½"

B?

Date 1778: probably by Pack & Chapman of London. Cf. Glenbervie, etc., also Session Records:—

"1778. 9th Augt. The Minister presented acct. of new bell for new Kirk fully dischd. by Capt Valentine.
Ballance or difference in exchange betwixt the old and new bell   £4 : 4 : 0
Shore dues and other incidental expenses 5/6."

"1779. Janr. 24th For *stocking* the new bell   £1 : 2 : 0
Up-putting of bell   3 : 0

Having become badly cracked, it was sold by the Heritors in 1896 for £2 11s.

Chapel of S.   ?   BALHAGERTY.
NO BELL.
Site doubtful.

Mains of DAVO.   1.

1 8 1 5

18½"

Probably by T. Mears of London.
In square bell-cot over S. side of farm buildings which are dated 1812.
Used as a clock bell; no longer rung.

GLENBERVIE.   S. Michael.

NO BELL.
Very little of the old church left.

Established Church.   1.

1 7 8 9

18"

Probably by W. & T. Mears of London. Lip filed away ½ in. on one side, ¼ in. on other, to allow of swinging in present belfry when it was brought from old church on the building of this one in 1826.
In small bird-cage belfry over W. end.
10 a.m., s. 11 a.m.
The tradition that Drumlithie Town bell came from here is dealt with below.

Chapel of S. Mary.   DILLAVAIRD.
NO BELL.
Site doubtful.

? Chapel of S. Conon.   **DRUMLITHIE.**
NO BELL.
Site doubtful.

Episcopal Church of S. John-the-Baptist.   **DRUMLITHIE.**

1 8 3 4

14⅞"
One canon broken. Probably by T. Mears of London.   2 qrs. 18 lbs.

In S. arch of double arch belfry at W. end : used to be in old church, the belfry of which is now preserved in the Rectory garden.

See also *Town Steeple*.

Free Ch.   1.
on soundbow
J WARNER & SONS LONDON 1868

17⅞"
1 cwt. 2 qr.

In arch belfry over W. end. The "Kirk lum" finds an outlet through the sill of the belfry immediately underneath the bell!

Town Steeple.   **DRUMLITHIE.**
on waist

1868

/   15⅜"
A flower-pot bell with a large projecting lip and no soundbow. Recast in Dundee from one by John Mowat of Old Aberdeen.

There is a tradition that the old town bell of Drumlithie came from Glenbervie Church ; if so, it must have been an earlier bell than the predecessor of the one there now (d. 1789), for it is known to have been hanging in a tree prior to 1777, when the old steeple was built.

The most probable explanation is that the bell was taken away from Glenbervie with the church plate after the Revolution for use at the Episcopal Church in Drumlithie, that it was broken by Cumberland in 1746, recast for use as a "town's bell" by the inhabitants (who were then all Episcopalians), and hung in a large ash tree in the middle of the village. This would correspond with the fact of the old bell having been one of Mowat's. It was put into the old steeple when that was built in 1777, and was broken by some boys in 1868, when it was recast and the new steeple was built.

The vane from the old steeple—a cock, dated 1777—is still preserved on an outhouse in the village, and the ash tree in which the bell used to hang is still flourishing.

6 a.m., 10 p.m. daily exc. Sundays.

INVERBERVIE.   **S. Mary.**

NO BELL.

Old bell : now in bell-cot on **Police Station** :—   1.

1 7 9 2   18"

Probably by T. Mears of London. Disused. Formerly rung at 6 a.m., 9 a.m., 2 p.m., and 9 p.m.

Established Ch. 1.

GIVEN BY PROVOST BARCLAY TO THE BURGH OF BERVIE 1791

on upper part of waist THOS MEARS OF LONDON FECIT

21½"

In tower at E. end.

Formerly the property of the town; the bell now on the Police Station was the bell of the old church till the new one was built in 1832, when an exchange was made with the town bell.

9 a.m., s. 11 a.m. [until 1872, also at 10.30 a.m., s. 12.]
The belfry of the old church is still standing.

Carmelite Church of S. ?
NO BELL.
Site only.

? KINGORNIE.   S. ?

Parish now included in KINNEFF.
NO BELL.
Site only.

KINNEFF.   S. Adamnan. 1.

§ PIETER + OSTENS HEEFT MY GEGOTEN TE ROTTERDAM · A°: 1 6 7 9

on waist   * M *
           * I * H *

§ Detached floral ornament: a small rose and leaves.
† Figure of recumbent ox.
* Small rose.

23"
1½

In a kind of bird-cage belfry over W. end.

11 a.m., s. 11.30.

The initials on the waist stand for "Master James Honeyman," in charge here from 1663 to 1693, in whose time the bell was obtained, as appears from Archbishop Sharp's "Visitation" entitled:—

"A Register of the Visitations of the severall Churches by and within the bounds of the Presbetry of the Mearns appointed by the Archbishope and Synod

Aprile 27th 1677."

in which the following occurs:—

"Kirk of Kinneff
June 26th 1678."

"Being asked concerning the Church it was answered, that the heritors had accorded for to make up its defects necessary for its intire reparation. Theirs no utensils nor bell for convocating of the people. The Minister is appointed to urge the heritors to supplie these wants......................"

"Master James Gavin, Clerk."

Chapel of S. John the Baptist.   **BARRAS.**
NO BELL.
Site only.

Free Ch.   ROADSIDE OF KINNEFF. 1.

PRESENTED TO THE FREE CHURCH OF KINNEFF BY JAS JOLLY

on upper part of waist   † 1851 †

† Floral ornament.
No canons.   about 15"

LAURENCEKIRK.   S. Laurence-the-Archbishop. 1.

VICKERS SONS & Cº SHEFFIELD FOR PATENT CAST STEEL 7880

§ Royal Arms.   24"

2 cwt. 1 qr. 2 lbs.

No canons; cast iron stock and wheel: hanging on cast iron brackets bolted to floor of open belfry at top of small campanile at W. end. No means of access. Obtained in 1895 when church was restored and enlarged.

Formerly rung at 8 a.m. and at 10 a.m.; recently the latter ringing was discontinued, but now it has been revived, and the former discontinued.

Old bell : —

By T. Mears of London, taken to Garvoc in 1895, *q.v.* p. 31. Used to hang in arch belfry over W. end.

Chapel of S. Anthony.   **CHAPELKNAP OF SCOTSTON.**
NO BELL.
Site only.

Episcopal Church of S. Laurence-the-Archbishop.   1.

T. MEARS OF LONDON FECIT 1813.

18½"

Originally in an inaccessible position at top of steeple: brought down and rehung in a lower stage by Mears & Stainbank of London in 1895.

MARYCULTER.   S. Mary.

NO BELL.

Very few remains of the church.

The bell was broken by some fishermen at a funeral about 100 years ago. It was one of three famous bells in the district, of which that of Trinity Chapel, Aberdeen, was another.

A few stones of the old belfry are left.

Established Ch.   1.

✠ Sancta · Maria · Ora · Pro · Nobis.

on waist

MEARS & STAINBANK. LOND. MDCCCXCVI.

20"

* Fleur-de-lys.
In bird-cage belfry over W. end.
Old bell :—

      1786   1787

The two dates are most peculiar: the bell is badly cracked, and is perhaps by an inferior English founder. It is now carefully preserved in the hall adjoining the church.

Church within St. Mary's College. BLAIRS.
Our Lady of the Assumption.

(1) *NO INSCRIPTION.*

(3) *above soundbow*   J MURPHY FOUNDER DUBLIN 1859   12"

20"

(3) A good bell with large canons, the faces of which have a reed ornament; crown flat, with mouldings, angular shoulders; waist separated from soundbow by a small band of moulding; no beads; clapper very large and heavy.

In round tower between N. Front and W. wing.

(a) Disused; hangs on iron brackets at S. side of chimney-stack in centre of main buildings. It may be very old.

Free Ch.   1.
NO INSCRIPTION.
A diminutive bell without interest.

MARYKIRK.   S. Mary.

NO BELL.
Very few remains of the church.
The bell is said to have been broken by a stone from one of "Butcher" Cumberland's men. Whether this is true is rather doubtful, as it is hardly likely that it would have been removed to the new church in an injured state.

Established Ch.   1.

1 8 2 6

17¼"
Recast by T. Mears of London.   said to be 2 cwt.
In arch belfry at S. end.
10 a.m., formerly also at 9 a.m., s. 11 a.m.

One Sunday while the previous bell was cracked, the precentor handed the minister a paper requesting the prayers of the congregation on behalf of "Mary Bell in great distress." This the minister read out, believing that it referred to a sick parishioner. If the bell was called "Mary," as this seems to imply, it must almost certainly have been a Mediaeval, in which case it must also have been the bell that is said to have been broken in 1746.

Chapel of S. Middanus.   INGLISMALDIE.
NO BELL.
Site doubtful.

? Chapel of S. John.   BALMANNO.
NO BELL.
Sites doubtful.

Episcopal Church.   ROSEHILL.
NO BELL.
Church desecrated.

36   BELLS OF KINCARDINESHIRE.

United Presbyterian Ch.				LUTHERMUIR.	1.
NO INSCRIPTION.
A diminutive bell without interest.
The only U.P. bell in the county.

Free Ch.										1.
            JOHN DUFFUS & Cº ABERDEEN. 1880
                                                                    11¼"
No canons : lettering very irregular.

Thornton Castle.									1.
            J: TAYLOR & Cº FOUNDERS 1879.
                                                                    20¾"
Denison headed.   2 cwt. 3 lbs.
In bell-cot on stables, used as clock bell. Was put here by Alex. Crombie, Esq., when he rebuilt the stables.

## NEUDOS. S. Drostane.							1.
Parish now included in FETTERCAIRN and in EDZELL.
NO BELL.
Hardly anything left except the churchyard.

## NIGG. S. Fiachra.								1.
    JOHN ‡ MOWAT OLD † ABD ⁑ ME FE IT 1759IN U UMECCLESIÆ · DE NIGG
    SABATA PANGO FUNRA PLANGO § §..............
                    ....   17¼"
    ‖ ‖......Ornamental border
    § §......same inverted
    ⁑ Scrap of lower border
    † same inverted
Numerous blunders and irregularities. Read "ferit" and "usum" for "fe it" and "u um."
Church in ruins.
In bird-cage belfry over E. end.   Disused.

Chapel of S. Fotinus.					TORRY.
NO BELL.
Site doubtful.

Established Ch.									1
            JOHN BLAIKIE & SONS ABERDEEN 1833 FECIT
                                                                    25"
In tower at N. end.
11 a.m., s. 12, s. 6 p.m.

BELLS OF KINCARDINESHIRE.

| Chapel within H.M. Prison. | CRAIGINCHES. | 1. |

on soundbow J WARNER & SONS LONDON 1890

In arch belfry.

3 qrs.

| Episcopal Church of S. Mary-the-Virgin. | COVE. | 1. |

on crown 20
on soundbow   J . WARNER & SONS . LONDON . 1890.

10¼"
1 qr. 2 lbs.

No canons.
In iron frame over E. [W.] end,

| "East Coast Mission." | COVE. | 1. |

NO INSCRIPTION.

14"
2 qrs.

No canons.   Cast by J. Blaikie & Sons of Aberdeen in 1887.

| Free Ch. | TORRY. | 1. |

J. BLAIKIE . AND . SONS 1890

20½"
2qrs. 12 lbs.

Lettering irregular and in high relief.
Given by Mr. Peter Johnstone, Fish Salesman.
In turret at N.W. corner.

S.ᵀ CYRUS.   S. Cyricus.   3.

(1) C & G MEARS FOUNDERS LONDON 1847

16½"

(2) C & G MEARS FOUNDERS LONDON 1846

21½"

(3) C & G MEARS FOUNDERS LONDON 1847

25"
3 cwt. 2 qrs. 12 lbs.

Nos. 1 and 2 are clock bells, and were obtained by Bryson of Edinburgh, who supplied the clock.   They are now disused.   No. 3 was recast from the old bell, which was inscribed :—

W & T MEARS LATE LESTER PACK & CHAPMAN OF LONDON FECERUNT 1789

abt. 24½
3 cwt. 1 qr. 14 lbs.

The 3rd is rung at 10 a.m., s. 11 a.m.; [? formerly also rung at 8 a.m.]
All hang in tower below spire at N. end.

| Chapel of S. Laurence-the-Archbishop. | LAURISTON. |

NO BELL.
Site only.

Chapel of S. Regulus.
NO BELL.
Site only.

MORPHIE.

? Chapel of S.   ?
NO BELL.
Site only.

FOREBANK OF CANTERLAND.

Free Ch.   1.
NO INSCRIPTION.

$17\frac{1}{4}''$

No canons. Very much like the bell of Johnshaven Free Church, *q.v.*, p. 25.

Lauriston Castle.   1.
on crown   16 is.

MEARS & STAINBANK, FOUNDERS, LONDON, 1869.

$16\frac{3}{4}$

Hangs in an arch in battlemented parapet at the top of a modern addition to the old tower in the courtyard. Approached by stone newel staircase. An old bell, rather smaller, used to stand disused in the stables till a few years ago, when it was taken away to Montrose and sold with some scrap iron.

Ecclesgreig House.   1.
NO INSCRIPTION.

$10\frac{1}{4}''$

Long waist, foreign-looking soundbow, but shank head.
Used formerly to hang in a tree.

STRACHAN.   S. Mary.   1.

NO INSCRIPTION.

$13\frac{3}{4}$

A very peculiar bell fully treated of at p. 14. The oldest in the county; probably c. 1500. Was formerly in small belfry at W. end of old church. When the new church was built in 1866, the bell was hung in a large beech tree outside the S.W. corner of the old churchyard. It was used at funerals till it was taken out of the tree in 1895. It is now in the Session House adjoining the church, where it was put for preservation in 1896.

Established Ch.
NO INSCRIPTION (?)

19"
1 cwt. 12½ lbs.

Inaccessible; cast by Bowen of Clerkenwell in 1890.
In arch belfry at S. end.
10.30 a.m., s. 11.30.

Free Ch. 1.
NO INSCRIPTION.
A diminutive bell without interest.

A specimen of a Seventeenth century English ornamental border[1] for comparison with the Low Country work of the same date.

[1] Used by the Bagleys of Northampton. The block was very kindly lent by Mr. A. H. Cocks of Gt. Marlow, Bucks.

BELFRIES.

I. SCOTLAND GENERALLY.

During the middle ages in Scotland, it seems to have been the exception and not the rule for the average country church to have a tower. Notwithstanding this, however, the Mediaeval builders do not appear to have been contented with the mere single-arch bell-gable that sufficed for the smaller churches in England, but gradually developed a more elaborate type of belfry almost peculiar to Scotland, a type, moreover, which survived the Reformation, and lived on long after all traces of artistic feeling had been eliminated from nearly every other class of ecclesiastical stonework. Although numbers have perished at the hands of niggardly heritors, many belfries of more or less interest still remain, several indeed having been carefully preserved from previous churches. The varied and beautiful forms which these little erections often assume even on buildings otherwise plain to ugliness and unworthy of notice, give ample reason for devoting some share of attention to them.

The average Scotch Mediaeval belfry was something like a very small "saddle-back" tower, open at each end and partly closed at the sides. Examples of this kind are to be seen at Abdie in Fifeshire, Dyce and Auchindoir in Aberdeenshire and Corsraguel (for two bells) in Ayrshire. Occasionally they were like elaborate arch bell-gables, and sometimes they were miniature towers with pinnacles, &c.

When the Rennaissance came, it did not alter the forms of the belfries, but merely clothed them in "classical" dress. This is clearly shown by such examples as Kinneff and Nigg. Of the later belfries, the best specimens are to be found near the east coast. Aberdeenshire is peculiarly rich in them—indeed those of Insch, Leslie, and Pitsligo are really most remarkable specimens of Rennaissance carving. We may attribute much of the excellence of the east coast belfries to Low Country influence, as many of them have a distinctly foreign appearance; in fact it is said that the stones for Pitsligo were brought from Holland in 1636. That there was constant communication with Holland we know for a fact, and as all the best bells came from there, it is not unnatural to suppose that the belfries also received a share of foreign influence.

The great majority of these belfries fall under the open stonework class that we may perhaps be allowed to call the "bird-cage" type, in view of the following considerations. A characteristic feature of the churches in the Thames valley and its immediate neighbourhood is formed by the pepper-box erections on the tops of so many of the towers. These are open woodwork cages that were put up during the Rennaissance period for the reception of the clock bell—a very usual addition to the ordinary peal. They are of little interest in themselves, and are usually only remarkable for the magnificent vanes with which they are almost always surmounted. In outline, however, they bear a sort of general resemblance to the Scotch stone belfries, especially when seen from a distance. As the author is under the impression that he has seen the term "bird-cage belfry" applied to them, he has in this present

INVERBERVIE (OLD CHURCH)   KINNEFF   GARVOC.

work ventured to apply it to the belfries under consideration for want of a more suitable term.

All the really good belfries seem to have been at one time surmounted by vanes, and indeed we may almost say that when the vane went, the belfry followed; for towards the end of the last century we see the vane and the artistic details vanishing together; and with the spurious "gothic" (?) revival of about seventy years ago, the belfry was supplanted by the wooden frame or the modern arch.

II. KINCARDINESHIRE.

The two circular turrets at Arbuthnott are the only Mediaeval belfries left in Kincardineshire, if we except the cill of one at the west end of the ruined church in Dunnottar Castle. This last seems to have formed part of a small square belfry something like that at Dyce. The Arbuthnott turrets are unusual; they are decidedly unecclesiastical, being in fact identical with the domestic work of the period. There is not the slightest attempt at ornamentation, and both are finished off with rough conical stone roofs, each terminating in a ball. They were built by Sir Robert Arbuthnott in 1505, at the time when he built the Arbuthnott Chapel on the south side of the chancel. The belfry attached to the chapel is in the angle between the west wall of the chapel and the south wall of the church; the lower part of it contains the stone newel staircase leading to the chamber above the chapel, while the upper part probably held two bells. It is semi-octagonal as far as a large rounded stringcourse at the level of the chapel wall-plate, above which it is circular. The other turret is in the centre of the west end of the church and contains the bell. It takes the form of a semi-hexagonal projection from the wall broken by a string about half way up, below which is a small ogee-headed niche: just beneath the level of the roof-ridge it is corbelled out at the sides and becomes circular. Access to the bell is obtained by raising a ladder inside the church to a small square-headed doorway high above the floor, from which a few steps in the thickness of the wall lead into a chamber at the very top of the turret.

Of the post-reformation belfries, the earliest is possibly that of Garvoc, which is said to have been preserved in 1778 from the previous church of a hundred years earlier. It is made of the black trap rock from the Hill of Garvoc, and is of peculiarly quaint design: the treatment of the pillars is very bold and effective. It is surmounted by a good weathercock, and is the best piece of work of the kind in Kincardineshire.

The west wall of Kinneff seems to belong to a much earlier date than the rest of the church, which was largely rebuilt in 1734, and the belfry may date from about 1679, when the present bell was obtained, although it is more probably later. It is a small square tower built of rustic ashlar work, open at each end, but except for a sort of pigeon-hole to receive the bell-bearings, closed at the sides. The roof is pyramidal and has good mouldings; a vase-shaped finial takes the place of the usual ball. There are the remains of a vane at the top, and the whole is an excellent Renaissance version of the usual Mediaeval type. The moss-grown stones and the grass on the top make it an exceedingly picturesque object.

F

The belfry on the ruined church at Fetteresso is dated 1737, and is something between those of Nigg and Kinneff; it is chiefly noticeable for the small pseudo-gables at the top, from the middle of which rises a long thin stone shaft seemingly intended to support a ball and vane.

The next in point of date is that of Nigg, remarkable for being on the east end of the church. On the die is the following inscription[1]:—

$$\begin{array}{c} \text{M} \\ [\text{R}] \quad \bullet \quad \text{M} \\ \text{MINISTER} \\ 1704 \end{array}$$

There is a very good pennon vane dated 1763, and a pretty double fleur-de-lys north-point. The body of the belfry is of a kind by no means uncommon, and is probably of the same date as the vane. Other examples, almost identical, will be found at Birse, Kincardine O'Neil, and Kettins. The treatment of the roof is particularly happy; the ornaments are evidently gothic pinnacles classicised. A like treatment, only more crudely carried out, may be found at Midmar (New Church) 1788, and a very elaborate extension of the same idea may be seen at Birse.

In the old churchyard at Maryculter are lying some stones which undoubtedly formed part of the belfry of the old church. Although rather mutilated, they show that it must have been very like the one at Nigg, only with a very prominent roll moulding at each angle.

The old belfry at Bervie is perhaps the most elegant of any in the county. It consists of four square fluted pillars with carved capitals supporting a tapering roof, which ends in a ball with the remains of a vane. It differs from all the rest in having no stone supports for the bell, which was hung on an iron frame.

Dunnottar, dated 1782, shows a well-proportioned example of the extremely plain kind: a very late example with small pinnacles has been preserved from the old Episcopal Church at Drumlithie.

The remainder of the "bird-cage" belfries in the county are all more or less debased examples not worth mentioning at length; they are at Maryculter (1787), Durris (1822), Banchory Devenic (1822, with a good cock and arrow vane), Glenbervie (1826), Benholm (1832), and Porthlethen *q.s.* (1856). Marykirk and Strachan have modern arch belfries. Fetteresso (1810), Banchory Ternan (1824), Fordoun (1829), Nigg Established Church (1829), Bervie (1837) have modern towers. Fettercairn (1830), St. Cyrus (1853), and Laurencekirk (1896) have small modern spires. Drumtochty and Stonehaven Episcopal Churches have good modern campaniles, and Drumlithie Episcopal Church has a double-arch belfry.

The quaint old Town Steeple of Stonehaven must not be forgotten. It was built by subscription in 1797, and consists of a square tower surmounted by a short octagonal wooden spire covered with copper. The tower is of the plainest kind, and the top is surmounted by a wooden railing. There is a good weathercock on the spire.

---

[1] The letters stand for "Master Richard Maitland," minister of Nigg from 1673 to 1719.

The town bell of Drumlithie used formerly to hang in a tree, but a miniature steeple was built for it in 1777. This was rebuilt in an enlarged form in 1868. It consists of a narrow cylindrical stone tower surmounted by a kind of small bird-cage belfry terminating in a thin spirelet, the whole being capped by an elaborate vane. Although the stonework is of the plainest possible order, and the total height not more than twenty feet, the effect is extremely quaint and picturesque. So far as is known to the writer, it is unique.

Of bells in trees there have been four instances in Kincardineshire, viz :—at Fettercairn, Drumlithie, Ecclesgreig House, and Strachan, all of which have been mentioned above.[1] This practice of hanging bells in trees seems to have been by no means unusual in Scotland ; in times past there were other instances at St. Monance, Auldbar, and Navar, to mention only a few.

[1] pp. 28, 32, 38.

APPENDIX.

I.

The author believes the following places to be possessed of Mediaeval bells; as his information, however, is very defective, he mentions them here in the hope of eliciting further particulars regarding them.

Manor,	Peebles-shire,	1478.
Dundonald,	Renfrewshire,	1485.
Linlithgow,	Linlithgowshire,	1490.
Broxburn,	Linlithgowshire,	1503.
Turriff,	Aberdeenshire,	1556.
Auchterarder,	Perthshire,	?

II.

Books have been published at various times giving full particulars of all the bells in each of the following counties:—

Bedfordshire,	by	Thos. North.
Buckinghamshire,	,,	A. H. Cocks.
Cambridgeshire,	,,	Rev. J. J. Raven, D.D.
Cornwall,	,,	E. Dunkin.
Devonshire,	,,	Rev. H. T. Ellacombe.
Gloucestershire,	,,	,,
Hertfordshire,	,,	Thos. North; completed by J. C. L. Stahlschmidt.
Kent,	,,	J. C. L. Stahlschmidt.
Leicestershire,	,,	Thos. North.
Lincolnshire,	,,	,,
Norfolk,	,,	H. L'Estrange.
Northamptonshire,	,,	Thos. North.
Rutland,	,,	,,
Somersetshire,	,,	Rev. H. T. Ellacombe.
Staffordshire,	,,	Chas. Lynam.
Suffolk,	,,	Rev. J. J. Raven, D.D.
Surrey,	,,	J. C. L. Stahlschmidt.
Sussex,	,,	W. D. Amherst Tyssen.

It is believed that the following will soon be forthcoming:—

Essex. Nearly completed by the late J. C. L. Stahlschmidt; said to be now in the press.

Derbyshire. Begun by the late Llewellyn Jowett; now being completed by W. H. St. John Hope (?)

Middlesex. Investigation just begun.

Northumberland. Said to be under investigation.

Shropshire.	,,	,,
Wiltshire.	,,	,,

ANOTHER VIEW.

PART OF THE FRAME REMOVED TO SHOW THE BELL.

A TYPICAL MODERN ENGLISH BELL WITH THE USUAL HANGINGS.

III.
EXPLANATION OF TECHNICAL TERMS.

In the bell depicted on the opposite page the following points should be carefully noted:
The angular projections forming the uppermost piece of the bell, by which it is hung, are called the canons (Lat. *ansa*).

The top of the bell, from which the canons project, is called the CROWN.

The convex part between the crown and the inscription is called the SHOULDER (Lat. *cerebrum* vel *caput*); this is the thinnest part of the bell.

The convex part at the base of the bell is called the SOUNDBOW; this is the thickest part, and the clapper ought always to strike upon it.

The edge of the bell at the mouth is called the LIP (Lat. *labium*).

The middle part of the bell between the soundbow and the shoulder is called the WAIST.

In this case the inscription is carried round the bell just below the shoulder; this is the usual place for it, and it is between two sets of BEADS, WIRES, or LINES.

When the HEAD of a bell is mentioned, it is not a translation of the Latin *caput*, which means the shoulder, but it indicates the part of the bell by which it is hung, be it canons, shank, "Denison-head" (a species of canons), or merely the middle of the crown.

The wooden block to which the bell is hung is called the STOCK. At the ends of the stock on its under side are fastened very strong steel pins or axles known as the GUDGEONS. These receive the whole weight of the bell, and work in gun-metal bearings which are let into cast-iron pedestals bolted to the frame, and are covered with caps to keep out the dust. The lubricant ought to be the best lard, which has to be softened with a little oil in frosty weather.

The upright piece of wood at the left hand side of the stock is called the STAY. It is used when the bell is "up" to keep it from falling over, by coming in contact with the SLIDER. This is the wooden bar which can be seen in the illustrations working on a pivot fixed to one side of the frame below the bell. The end of the slider is free to slide—hence the name—along the frame on the other side for such a distance as may allow the stay to rest against it on whichever side the bell is turned.

The reader should notice the peculiar form of the wheel and the arrangement of the rope, as all large bell-wheels are exactly alike in form. Each part of the wheel has its name, but as wheels are so little used in Scotland, it would be needless to say more about them.

English bells have been hung like this, with but slight variation, for the last two hundred years, and the same method is still followed in the majority of cases. It is true that modifications have been introduced of late years, such as iron frames and iron stocks, as shown in the picture of the Aberavon peal, but they are by no means universally used.

IV.

The following extracts relating chiefly to the St. Cyrus bells are from some papers which the writer was enabled to examine through the kindness of the Rev. Robert Davidson, the Minister of the Parish. It is hoped that they will be found of sufficient interest to justify their insertion here.

"CANTERLAND,
18th August, 1846."

"DEAR SIR,

When I received your note last week I was not aware of anything to prevent my attending the meeting on the 29th, but I now find that I shall be otherwise unavoidably engaged on that day, and I shall therefore give you all the information I have about Bells.

The first which came in my way was that of Marykirk, and when it was broken, Mr. Napier, a native of the parish and a merchant in London, happened to be in the county and took charge of procuring a new one from Mears, the celebrated Bell-founder of Whitechapel. The next was that of Laurencekirk, which was managed in the same way, Mr. Napier having also taken the trouble of getting it at my request. When a large new bell was to be got for Fordoun I recommended it to be ordered from the same Bell-founder in London. The late Dr. Crombie of Thornton, who was then the principal Heritor of the Parish took the trouble of selecting it when in London, and was at some pains to choose one of a good tone.

The Vouchers of the expense have been out of my hands a long time, and I can only give you an idea of it from imperfect recollection.

The bells for Marykirk and Laurencekirk were each something above 1 cwt., and they cost somewhere about 1 6 ℔ lib., but were at different prices probably owing to the price of metals being different at the respective periods. The value given for the old bells was also different, and was about 7d. or 8d. ℔ lib.

The Fordoun bell was between 5 and 6 cwt., and cost I think about 1/8 or 1/9 ℔ lib., so far as I can recollect. The old bell was sold for another Church. The probable cost of a new bell for St. Cyrus may therefore be estimated at about 1/- ℔ lib. if of the same weight as the old bell after allowing for the old metal. The stock, wheel, and iron work are charged separately.

As Mr. Lyall of Lauriston is so frequently in London perhaps he may be so kind as to take the trouble of getting the new bell, and if he should not have a musical ear like Dr. Crombie, who told me he spent nearly a day ringing a great number of bells in Mears' Foundry in order to select one to strike a proper note, Mr. Lyall could possibly get someone in London to assist him.

I enclose Mears' Shop Bill of 1835, the only evident I can now find on the subject, but I see from my accounts I remitted him £58 1/8 for the Fordoun bell."

"Yours truly,
J. PETER."

"THE REV. J. S. MURRAY."

The following will show that the present bell of St. Cyrus is much smaller than was originally intended :—

" BELLFOUNDRY, WHITECHAPEL,
January 14th, 1847."

"SIR,

Mr. Lyall has called this day respecting the bell for St. Cyrus, and has chosen one of 7 to 8 cwts.—on our recommendation—he requested us to inform you that he had decided on the bell, and also that he wished you to forward the old one to us by the first vessel.

If any name is to be put on the bell he wished us to request you to send it up as soon as possible."

"We are, Sir,

"Mr. J. A. MURRAY."
Yours very truly,
CHAS. & GEO. MEARS."

As an account is in existence headed "Expense of recasting and erecting Parish Church Bell of St. Cyrus, &c.," the above letter merely indicates that Mr. Lyall chose the *size* and not the actual bell.

It may be assumed that the disused clock bells were obtained by Bryson of Edinburgh, who supplied the clock, as the following is the only reference to anything of the kind that can be found :—

"Mr. JAMES MURRAY, &c., &c., *St. Cyrus* by Montrose." "BRIDGE OF ALLAN, By Stirling, 16th August, 1847."

"DEAR SIR,

. . . . The clock originally ordered from Messrs. Bryson was declared by them to be a first rate one, and appropriate for the purpose and situation—if therefore Miss Watson's Trustees want something *better than good* to strike the *quarters*, &c., &c., it will be simply absurd—since very few will be the better for such needless outlay."

"R. LYALL."

BELL FOUNDRY, WHITECHAPEL, LONDON, April 20, 1848.

J. A. Murray, Esq.
To CHAS. & GEO. MEARS.

1847.					
Feb. 12.	Charges paid on Old Bell,	...	£0	4	6
1848.					
Mar. 23.	A Bell 3 cwt. 2 qr. 12 lb. at 7s. ℔ cwt.,	...	25	5	0
	Clapper, ...	...	1	0	0
	Stock, Gudgeons, Ironwork and Brasses,	...	2	12	6
	Wharfage, ...	...	0	2	6
			£29	4	6

	cwt.	qr.	lb.				
By Old Bell,	3	1	14				
Deduct Iron Staple and dirt,	0	0	4				
Cwt.	3	1	10 @ £4 4s. ℔ cwt., ...	...	14	0	6
					£15	4	0

58 lb. of iron to the St. Cyrus Church Bell,	...	0	19	6
Repairs on the rest of the iron, ½ ...	...	1	0	0
8 lb. of Old Bell Mettel at 6d., ...	...	0	4	0
		£0	16	0

Bell Acct. Blacksmith Work [signed] DAVID MILNE.

(The "Bell Mettel" probably refers to the broken canons of the old bell.)

Mr. James Murray, pro. the Parish of St. Cyrus.   LINKS FOUNDRY, MONTROSE.

To JACK & KERR.

1848.					
May 19.	To a Cast iron Wheel for Parish Bell, 1 cwt. c14 Rt.,	...	£0	17	6
,,	,, a pattern for Wheel, Wood and Work, ...	...	0	12	0
,,	,, Man's time at St. Cyrus assisting to fit up wheel,	...	0	3	0
,,	,, 4 Bolts for fastening Wheel together. ...	...	0	0	8
			£1	13	2
May 19.	By Old Wheel, weighing 1 cwt. 1 qr. c2/ Rt.,	...	0	2	6
			£1	10	8

V.

IRISH AND ENGLISH FOUNDRIES.

The following notes on the history of the chief Irish and English foundries which have sent bells to Scotland may be found of interest as showing to some extent the position of bell-founding at the present day. For a great part of them the author is indebted to several of the English books, especially those of North and Stahlschmidt. Mention has been made of some of the most noticeable specimens of modern bell-founding, and the writer has attempted to give representative examples from each part of Scotland. For obvious reasons, any criticism of their respective merits is out of the question, and an alphabetical arrangement has been followed as far as possible, seeing that all the foundries mentioned are still in existence.

IRELAND.

So far as is known to the writer, the ancient founders, such as Tobias Covey for example, are unrepresented in Scotland, and the only Irish foundry that need be mentioned seems to be the comparatively modern one of John Murphy of Dublin, which was started in 1816, and has done a great amount of work for Ireland. It is represented in Scotland by the bells of Crieff Free Church (12 cwt., 1882); St. John's (R.C.), Fauldhouse (1882); Prestonkirk (13 cwt., 1884); Maybole Town Hall (20 cwt., 1895); Falkirk Free Church (16 cwt., 1895), and by several others. This foundry has turned out some very large bells, among them those of Mullingar; S. Patrick's (R.C.), Dungannon (2 tons, 1889); S. Patrick's (R.C.), Wicklow (2 tons, 1890), and also several very heavy peals, as at Clogher; Belfast (10; tenor, 3 tons, 66 in., 1885), &c. These Irish bells form the opposite extreme from those of the Low Countries, being perhaps the heaviest in proportion to their size of any modern bells.

ENGLAND.
BRISTOL.

A peal of 10 at the Orphan Homes of Scotland, Tibbingshill, and single bells at Broughton and Glenrinnes are by Llewellins & James, general founders and engineers, who have taken to bell-founding recently.

CROYDON.

10 (tenor, 14 cwt.) "dead" bells at Kirkcaldy (1880), 5 at Paisley Town Hall (1882), 6 at Greenock Free Middle Church, 11 at Largs, 6 at Logie (1896), and many single bells are by Gillett & Johnston of Croydon, an old firm of clockmakers, who have only been casting bells since 1877.

LONDON: *Spitalfields*.

11 at Inverness Cathedral, 6 at Renton, and a few more, are by John Warner & Sons of Spitalfields. We first hear of this firm in 1740 when Jacob Warner, a Quaker, was ordered by the Founders Company to cease foundry work, on the ground that he was only free of the Tin-plate Workers. His son, John Warner, was in business as a bell and brass founder in 1763 at a house known as *the 3 bells and a star*, in Wood Street, Cheapside, where he was joined by Tomson Warner, his brother. Afterwards they moved to Fore Street, Cripplegate, and dissolved partnership in 1782. Tomson remained in Fore Street, while John went to Fleet Street in 1784, where as "John Warner & Sons" he cast bells, sometimes putting his own name on them and sometimes that of the firm. It was from Tomson Warner that the business descended to the present firm of John Warner & Sons. Prior to 1850 they only cast bells in sand, and less than 18 in., in diameter. Until a few years ago their foundry as

Peal of 8 bells (tenor 16 cwt.) for Aberavon Church, Glamorganshire.[1]

This is an example of an ordinary English peal constructed for change-ringing and shows some of the bells "up," ready for ringing. In this case the frame and stocks are of iron and the bells are without canons.

[1] By Messrs. J. Taylor & Co., of Loughborough, who kindly lent the block—which is from a photograph taken in their foundry.

well as their offices was at Jewin Crescent, Cripplegate—hence their foundry mark—but it has lately been removed to Spelman Street, Spitalfields. "Big Ben" was first cast by Warners.

LONDON : *Whitechapel.*

About 1570 one Robert Mot, whose father John Mott of Canterbury was busy in 1553 buying up old metal from churches, started a foundry on the north side of High Street, Whitechapel, on the site of Tewkesbury Court. Bell-founding was then just recovering from the Reformation, and Mot had abundance of work. In 1606 he sold the foundry to Joseph Carter, one of a Reading line of founders. Mot died in 1608. Carter, who died two years later, had meanwhile sent his son to London, leaving his interest in the Reading foundry to William Yare. William Carter the son died in 1619, and was replaced by Thomas Bartlet, who carried on the London business till 1647 when it passed to Anthony Bartlet, who in turn was succeeded by James Bartlet in 1676. The two last cast most of the bells for the London churches after the Great Fire. James Bartlet was followed in 1701 by Richard Phelps, who cast the five-ton clock bell of S. Paul's. He was succeeded by his foreman, Thomas Lester, who, following his predecessor's example, also took his foreman into partnership in the person of one Thomas Pack. This was in 1752. Lester built the present foundry on the south side of High Street, Whitechapel, a few yards east of the Parish Church of S. Mary Matfelon. He died in 1769 having provided in his will that Pack should receive his nephew William Chapman as a partner. He cast "Great Dunstan" at Canterbury Cathedral (3½ tons), and the peal of 12 at S. Mary-le-bow, Cheapside—the famous "Bow Bells" –(tenor, 53 cwt.), all in 1762. The bells in hand at Lester's death were inscribed "Lester, Pack & Chapman." Pack & Chapman cast among many others the peal of 12 at Wakefield Cathedral, and the 11 cwt. tenor at Brechin Cathedral. Pack died in 1781, and Chapman, who survived him three years, admitted as his partner William Mears. There are a very few bells cast by Chapman alone, and among them is the 1st of Stirling. In 1787 Thomas Mears became associated with William in the firm which was then designated " W. & T. Mears, late Lester, Pack & Chapman." William Mears having retired in 1789, Thomas Mears was alone till 1804, when he assumed as partner his son Thomas Mears the younger, whom we also find alone from 1810 till 1844. Thomas Mears (the younger) cast "Great Tom" of Lincoln (5½ tons) in 1835, and was succeeded by Charles and George Mears, who cast "Great Peter" of York (10¾ tons) in 1845, the Bourdon bell of Montreal (11½ tons) in 1847, and recast "Big Ben" (13½ tons) in 1858. In 1859 the designation of the firm was altered to G. Mears & Co., a title which was retained till the introduction of Robert Stainbank in 1865. This necessitated a further and final change to Mears & Stainbank, under which style the firm still remains.

Mears & Stainbank are also the successors of the equally famous foundry of the Rudhalls of Gloucester ; the smaller foundries of Briant of Hertford, Dobson of Downham, Moore, Holmes & Mackenzie of Redenhall have also been absorbed in that of Whitechapel.

The following bells in Scotland, among many others, are from this foundry :—the peals of 8 at St. Andrew's, Edinburgh (tenor, 15 cwt.), 1788 ; 8 at St. Paul's, Dundee (tenor, 23 cwt.), 1872 ; 8 at Dundee Old Steeple (tenor, 20 cwt.), 1873 ; 8 at Lochee (tenor, 8 cwt.), 1872 ; 6 at Dunkeld (tenor, 7 cwt.), 1813 ; 3 at St. Andrews, 1807-9 ; and the single bells at Kilmarnock (12 cwt.), 1853 ; Kirkcudbright (12 cwt.), 1838 ; Hamilton (1⅓ cwt.), 1848 : Johnston (16 cwt.), 1847 ; Renfrew (23 cwt.), 1885 ; Paisley (22 cwt.), 1866 ; Leith (20 cwt.), 1843 ; South Leith (23 cwt.), 1894 ; Peterhead (10 cwt.), 1850 ; Inverness (9 cwt.). 1851 ; Brechin E. Free Church (20 cwt.), 1892 ; Auchterless (22 cwt.), 1895.

LOUGHBOROUGH.

Next to the Whitechapel Foundry that of Messrs. John Taylor & Sons, Loughborough, has sent more bells to Scotland than any other English foundry. We first hear of it in 1717 when some clockmakers named Thomas and John Eayre started a foundry at Kettering, which was closed about 1761. Thomas' brother Joseph Eayre went to St. Neots, where he began to cast bells about 1733. After his death this foundry was held by Thomas Osborn, his foreman and Edward Arnold, who soon, however, dissolved partnership (c. 1770), Arnold remaining at St. Neots, while Osborn set up at Downham Market. About 1801 he took William Dobson his grandson into partnership, who held the foundry alone from 1806 till in 1833 it was bought up by Mears of Whitechapel.

In 1781 Edward Arnold started a foundry at Leicester, keeping up that at St. Neots as well, in which he received as apprentice Robert Taylor, who succeeded him there, when the foundry was carried on in a large brick building in the Priory, built in the form of a bell. Taylor with his sons William and John moved to Oxford in 1821. In 1825, John went to Buckland Brewer near Bideford, where he built a foundry, returning, however, to Oxford in 1833. In 1840 he left Oxford for Loughborough, where his son and grandsons are still carrying on the business.

They cast "Great Paul" (16 tons odd); 21 at Manchester Town Hall (tenor, 8 tons odd); 16 at Worcester Cathedral (tenor, 12 cwt.); 10 at Newcastle Cathedral; the clock bell (46 cwt.) at Londonderry Guildhall.

Their work in Scotland includes the 57 cwt. hour bell at Glasgow University, the biggest bell in Scotland, and the 10 (tenor, 42 cwt.) of S. Mary's Cathedral, Edinburgh, the biggest peal. Also 9 at St. Mary's Cathedral, Aberdeen (tenor, 30 cwt.); 8 at Port of Menteith (tenor, 17 cwt.); 8 at Coats' U.P. Church, Paisley (tenor, 24 cwt.); and the bells of St. Margaret's, Bognie (11 cwt.); Boness (23 cwt.); and Castle Douglas (15 cwt).

SMETHWICK.

"Charles Carr" of the Woodlands Brass Foundry, Smethwick, which dates from 1864, cast the 31 cwt. clock bell of Marischal College, Aberdeen in 1895, also bells at Druimbeg and Stromness, and recast a 2¾ cwt. bell at Coupar Angus. The foundry of Blews of Birmingham was merged in this firm some years ago.

"Steel bells" by Vickers, Sons, & Co., formerly Naylor, Vickers & Co. of the river Don Works, Sheffield are at Trinity, Glasgow (6; tenor, 12 cwt., 45″); Grange Free Church, Kilmarnock (54″); St. Giles, Edinburgh (8; tenor, 13¼ cwt., 50″); Ecclefechan (3; tenor, 5¾ cwt., 34″); Rutherglen Town Hall (48″); Coatbridge Free Middle (48″). This firm has cast a great number of the "Steel bells" within the last half century including a 90″ bell for S. Peter's (R.C.), Hatton Garden, London, and several peals, among them St. Clement's, Hastings (8; tenor, 52″, 17¾ cwt.), and Hurst, near Ashton-under-Lyne (8; tenor, 19¾ cwt., 54″).

"Tubular Bells," by Harrington, Latham & Co., Coventry are at Scone, 1894, and (a single tube) at S. Margaret's (R.C.), Ayr, 1889.

www.ingramcontent.com/pod-product-compliance
Lightning Source LLC
Chambersburg PA
CBHW020252090426
42735CB00010B/1893